Freedom from Clutter

FREEDOM *from* CLUTTER

The Guaranteed, Foolproof, Step-by-Step Process to Remove the Stuff That's Weighing You Down

Mel Mason

with Andy Earle

Some names and identifying details have been changed to protect the privacy of individuals.

For permission requests or bulk orders, please reach out to Mel Mason via email (info@declutteringspaces.com) or visit declutteringspaces.com

ISBN 978-0-578-77669-9

To all the incredible friends, coaches, and mentors who have been with me for this journey.

You've made my light shine brighter.

Contents

Introduction

Overcoming the Clutter

We all have clutter we must routinely clear out before it takes over our environment. For you it might be your desk buried by papers, your garage brimming with moving boxes, your car waist-deep in takeout rubbish, or even your headspace littered with negative thoughts and emotional baggage. Whatever it is, many of us haven't seen the floor in years and the clutter is multiplying. Like dirt on a window, clutter builds up slowly over time and blocks the light.

One client came to me with a schedule packed airtight. She was downtrodden, frantic, and looking for a lifeline. At 27, she was working a job she didn't like, enduring a relationship filled with phony "I love you's," and lacking the ability to address the toxicity cluttered her external world. The light wasn't shining through her windows. So I challenged her to a simple exercise for thirty days.

She was skeptical, but soon she'd organized her office and gotten rid of a mountain of files. Then she turned her attention to the garage and had it gutted and cleared in a single weekend. What happened next was a total revolution. Her life flipped 180 degrees. She recognized her relationship was problematic and ended it. She sought a new job and was offered an 80% salary increase. Between jobs, she was able to take a three week trip out of the country.

A month later she was living a completely different life; one of abundance.

She'd cleaned off her dirty windows and the light was shining through brighter than ever.

How can you achieve results like that? What's the secret to decluttering your life? Maybe you've tried a thousand times to clear the mess, but clutter keeps coming back with a vengeance. Perhaps you can't bear getting rid of important items and the sentimental memories they represent. There is a simple explanation for why you're having these problems, and a simple approach to clear the clutter away.

My name is Mel and people call me the "Clutter Expert" because I've been teaching about clutter for over seven years, ever since I discovered the secret to solving the clutter problem for good. I learned how to keep clutter from coming back once you've cleaned it up. And I've got a simple formula for how to organize the chaos (see Chapter 6).

But I'm also going to push you to go deeper. Messy spaces are often a symptom of inner turmoil. So, while these pages contain many hacks on how to effectively clean your spaces, they also reveal methods for cleansing your body and soul along the way. By the end of this book, you'll realize there's a link between outer clutter and inner clutter and you'll have specific steps to make decluttering your environment easy.

You'll see evidence of improvement immediately. You'll see that you have the ability to overcome challenges, master the mess, and feel the warm sun start to shine through your dirty windows (or as I call it, the Divine Energy of the Universe radiating into your life).

Where Do I Even Start?

Many people feel overburdened by accumulated gifts, collector's editions of every comic book known to mankind, or their grown kids' old projects and trophies that take up most of the garage. We don't know what to do with it all and many of us seek outside help, renting storage space and hiring professional organizers to stash our things away. After years of build up, it's no wonder many of us feel decluttering is an insurmountable task!

I was in the same boat for years.

Growing up, I was a messy kid. You couldn't see the floor in my bedroom; there were two little paths from the door, one going to the bed and another to the desk. When people saw my mess, they saw the physical representation of my inner clutter. They weren't able to see what was happening inside, but they knew it wasn't peachy.

I experienced trauma and loss, the hardest moment being when I was fifteen and I discovered my older brother's body after he took his life. This caused me to spiral into a black hole. My feelings were cluttered and tumultuous. I was kicked out of high school for being a danger to myself and others and placed in a residential treatment center for adolescents. I lived away from my friends and family and hated every minute of it, fiercely resisting the staff at the treatment center.

That all changed the day my regular therapist went on vacation.

My substitute therapist was *awesome*. She lived nearby and asked me to join her at a local yoga studio. There, I met the owner of the studio, who took me under her wing and taught me about being present and addressing the causes of clutter in my life.

Even with all the mindfulness and meditation, I still felt trapped. I was caught in the rut that clutter had created within me. I went down many alleyways trying to find my center—I was going to be a Reiki Healer at 19, a yoga and martial arts teacher in my 20s, and I even tried a stable desk job to find the balance I was craving. But through it all, my life was not fulfilling me.

I was in a dark place. I felt trapped and suffocated in my marriage. I was floundering.

That's when I discovered a simple technique I call Allowing the Now. In my 30's, I put Allowing the Now into practice and began to notice massive shifts.

I quit the miserable desk job and took my first leap out on my own as a personal assistant. When that fell through after just two weeks, my boss cut me a check for the entire balance of my 1-year contract (over $50,000). I was suddenly free to pursue whatever I wanted, but what would I do?

The insight I needed came from an unlikely place: reality T.V.

The first time I saw an episode of the show *Hoarders* and witnessed normal-looking people living amid mountains of filth, I was fascinated. After all, my room had looked exactly the same when I was a teenager. I too had mountains of stuff with a small path leading from the door to the bed and another to the desk.

I noticed that, like me, the individuals on *Hoarders* suffered from both internal and external clutter. I understood the external clutter was a defense mechanism to protect them from inner turmoil. The endless tchotchkes functioned as layers of protection that the hosts ripped away with no care to the hoarder's emotions. The show's subjects were left bare and adrift in the world without their protective layer of stuff. They were worse off than before. No internal progress had been made, and I knew these hoarders would regress to their old habits as soon as the cameras stopped rolling.

Watching the show triggered an idea: I could help people escape the clutches of clutter, both inside and out.

The Truth About Decluttering

Decluttering is about more than just cleaning up your external environment. Cleaning my room once a week as a teenager didn't help because I had too much stuff and not enough space to store it all. Clutter accumulates when we fail to address what weighs on us. Sometimes, we ignore a bad habit like eating too much fast food. Other times, we try not to think about the elephant-sized knick-knack pile in the foyer. Unchecked, these unhealthy habits block out the light in our lives. The Divine Energy of the Universe can't shine through.

When we recognize and address these problems, the clutter begins to vanish.

The process itself isn't difficult. You need to address that which clutters your life and blocks the light from coming in. At this very moment, clutter may be taking up room in your life. There could be three broken microwaves in the attic or dog toys for a pet you don't even have. There are repressed emotions, resentments, and fears tucked away in a corner of your soul that you don't want to deal with. Clutter you've avoided your whole life might emerge in this process and it might frighten you. But there's nothing to fear. With a little work, it will get better. I promise.

And when the dust settles, and you see the floor unblocked by clutter, you will feel a relief, lightness, and control you haven't felt in ages.

Don't let the clutter snuff out your light. Wipe off those grimy windows and let the sunshine trickle in. In this book, I'll guide you through the process one step at a time. Let's begin.

Chapter 1

Clutter 101

Living in today's world you accumulate a lot of stuff. Every year your home and life gets crammed with knick knacks, gifts, memories, important documents, and priceless heirlooms. Soon, it can feel like you're drowning in clutter. No matter how frantically you clear things out, the junk piles up faster. The thought of decluttering makes you feel like you're bailing water out of a sinking ship, struggling to keep it afloat.

When most people talk about clutter, they are referring to the physical items that enter your possession and fill up empty space in your home. First, it's the cabinets and closets that overflow. Soon, there are boxes hidden under tables, desks, and beds. Meanwhile, every surface in the house seems to undergo a similar transformation, as papers, photos, artwork, souvenirs, books, collectibles, appliances, tools, art supplies, packages of food, half-finished projects, and family relics pile on top of each other. Eventually the floor is littered with detritus and strewn with I'll-get-to-that's.

But clutter is more complicated than most people realize. Computer desktops get cluttered with icons, calendars get cluttered with appointments, and heads get cluttered with thoughts. Clutter is much bigger than just the boxes in the basement or the old trophies in the attic. There are different categories of clutter that must be handled in different ways. The strategies that work for one type are often ineffective for another type.

If you don't understand how clutter works and what the types are, it's almost impossible to adequately address the root of your clutter problem and erase the clutter from your life.

In this chapter, I'll show you how clutter works, where the different types come from, and how to apply this knowledge directly to your life. I'll break down the two main types of clutter, External and Internal, and I'll explain the three subclasses for each category.

External Clutter

The first type of clutter is the junk we're all familiar with: The totaled car still in the driveway, the defunct JBL speakers from your radio days, or that drawer in the kitchen that has no purpose other than to give unwanted items a home. I call this External Clutter. But External Clutter can go beyond just boxes and antiques. It's any clutter that exists outside of your mind, including digital clutter and even excess body weight.

The people on the show *Hoarders* suffer from External Clutter because their homes and garages overflow with items. But so does a professional who is stressed at work because she feels like there are too many tasks to get done each day. Her calendar is packed with clutter. The same is true of someone carrying around extra pounds on their body. Their diet is crammed with junk, and it's cluttering up their waistline.

When I was a kid, I had my own icefield of External Clutter to navigate. I never saw the floor of my bedroom apart from a deer-trail from the bed to the door. For many years I thought organization simply wasn't for me. I was wrong.

By the time I reached my mid twenties, I'd realized something important: We all have access to organization, we just need to remove the interference. At the time, I had interference in my life preventing me from decluttering. I had an aggravating job managing a bunch of crybabies, my wife was insomniac and kept me up all night in our tiny 600sqft apartment, and I didn't know I was putting up with an undiagnosed medical condition that prevented proper iron regulation (hemochromatosis). Long story short, I was *tired*.

My external life was in disarray, but I rolled up my sleeves and started to focus on getting my internal life straightened out. I took a hard look at myself and said, "Mel, put your happiness first." I knew what was possible because I'd been reading spiritual texts about self-care for years, but I hadn't yet actualized the principles I was learning. I was scared. I thought my problems were too big. It was more than I could take on by myself.

Turns out you don't have to take on your clutter by yourself. And you don't have to address it all at once. That's a limiting belief. I certainly didn't cancel my lease, divorce my wife, and quit my job all on the same day. That would be insane! But I did take mindful, tangible steps towards getting there. I took one step at a time.

For example, once I realized my job was a source of External Clutter that was interfering with my life, I started pausing at the beginning of each workday and sitting in my car outside the office for five minutes before going inside. It was the only place where I could find time completely to myself. I spent that time being thankful for my day, my body, and my life. It's this kind of attention that will help you organize your inner and outer mess.

There are three main classes of External Clutter: Physical Clutter consists of the items that pile up, Digital Clutter is the bits and bytes of data, and Body Clutter refers to the extra pounds of body weight that accumulate no matter how often you jog.

Let's explore each of these in more detail.

Physical Clutter (AKA "Stuff" or "Junk")

The first and most obvious type of External Clutter is Physical Clutter. This refers to the stuff most people think of as clutter. It's papers, artwork, musical instruments, furniture, photo albums, board games, clothes, pencils, and power tools. Any objects in your immediate environment can potentially be Physical Clutter when they start to stack up and overwhelm you.

One of my clients was a single woman with a huge three-bedroom house and two-car garage, and every last cabinet, cupboard, and closet was bursting at the seams. The garage had metal racks filled with gifts for any occasion, decorations for every season, and party supplies (just in case). Even the door handles were dripping in glass ornaments! I wanted to help her realize that a lot of this physical clutter was unnecessary.

I asked her about the boxes of pictures and memories in the garage. "How often do you look at those? How many do you really look at?" The answer was unsurprisingly, none of them. It was the same story for the dust-collecting décor and unused party favors, stored away but never looked at again. All of this stuff had turned into Physical Clutter.

What makes an object Physical Clutter? When something no longer brings you joy, it has become clutter and you should remove it from your life. If it still brings you joy, find a designated place for it. Useful objects with a good home aren't clutter.

Digital Clutter (AKA "Full Inboxes" and "Hard Drives")

The next class of External Clutter to be aware of is Digital Clutter. This can refer to anything that comes across your phone, computer, tablet, or TV screen. A prime example would be an overflowing inbox. Today, we are bombarded with notifications, likes, comments, and direct messages on a minute-by-minute basis. The constant onslaught of digital noise is a form of clutter. Because Digital Clutter occurs outside of your head, it's External Clutter.

Have you ever found yourself wondering how people used to fit everything on the generation 1 iPhone? We've moved from Megabytes to

Gigabytes to Terabytes in a short span of time, and no one has stopped to ask why we need so much space. We just accept that because we have more storage available, we should fill it up. Like a box of memories in the garage, if you don't look through your camera roll or messages from three years ago, it's not doing you any good on your phone, home computer, or cloud storage service.

Digital clutter can interfere with your life even if it doesn't take up physical space in your house. When you have a red notification for 12,724 unread emails, it's stressful! On a cluttered desktop, you might not be able to find the icon for the USB you just plugged in because it's buried in dozens of downloaded PDFs that you'll never open again.

Reducing Digital Clutter might require tossing your hard drive and starting fresh (copying over only the essentials) or using software to help put all the junk in one place. For example, I use an email client that puts all my subscriptions into one email so I can delete it with ease and keep my inbox clear, happy, and healthy.

Is every digital file, message, and post an instance of Digital Clutter? Certainly not. Your digital hoard only becomes a problem when it starts to weigh you down. With the icons on your desktop it's annoying and frustrating to find what you're looking for. But a curated album of photos from your trip to Tahiti might bring you loads of joy. It's saved in an unobtrusive location and does not weigh you down at all. That's digital gold, not clutter.

Body Clutter (AKA "Love Handles")

The third class of External Clutter, Body Clutter, is a constant worry for many people. Body Clutter refers to the extra weight many of us carry around everywhere we go. Every year we gain a few more pounds and pretty soon we've gone from supple to soft to saggy. Another form of Body Clutter is the use of drugs and alcohol. Anything about your body that blocks you from experiencing abundance and happiness is potentially a form of Body Clutter.

The Biggest Loser, a TV show that ran for 17 seasons and attracted an average 7.4 million viewers, became a staple in the weight loss world. Contestants on the show were led through intensive fat burning programs by fitness coaches and achieved remarkable results. It wasn't unusual for a contestant to shed 100 pounds in twelve weeks. However, when the curtains closed and these weight loss warriors returned home, their healthy habits didn't stick.

Without an environment to push contestants to maintain their goals, many fell back on cluttered schedules, meals, and workout routines that amounted to regaining lost weight. The contestants never learned how to pay proper attention to their bodies because the top fitness experts in Hollywood were doing it for them.

When you start putting on the love handles, you aren't being attentive to your health, and it manifests as external Body Clutter. By failing to regulate your diet and exercise, or by putting drugs into your system, you're cluttering up your body one poor decision at a time. However, it's never too late to declutter your body by showing yourself a little more respect. If you stay on top of your health, body clutter won't weigh you down.

This isn't to say that anyone who doesn't meet society's standards of body symmetry is cluttered. Extra pounds and unhealthy eating and drinking habits will only manifest as Body Clutter if you feel them weighing you down. If you're full-bodied and confident, you don't have anything to worry about. Reflect honestly about how you treat your body, and if it's bringing you joy, great. If not, start working to declutter your body.

Internal Clutter

If External Clutter is everything that happens outside of your head, then Internal Clutter involves the processes occurring within your skull. Thoughts and emotions have the power to weigh you down and block the Divine Energy of the Universe from flowing into your life. Anything in your head that's preventing you from experiencing abundance is a form of Internal Clutter. That could include negative self-talk, feelings of shame and unworthiness, or a bad attitude because you're having a tough week.

We all have some degree of Internal Clutter. We come into this world screaming and crying. Negative emotions are part of life from Day 1. Everyone can empathize with feelings of hurt and loss. Internal Clutter builds up when we let these negative feelings ruminate and multiply like weeds in a garden.

It's possible to tolerate a small dose of Internal Clutter in the same way it's possible to put off doing the dishes for a meal or two. But sooner or later, when the clutter stacks up too high, it can come crashing down and leave a nasty mess. Unlike dirty dishes, it's harder to gauge when your stack of Internal Clutter has reached critical mass. How can you assess your Internal Clutter levels and recognize the negative impact of leaving it unchecked?

When you're cluttered on the inside, you sabotage yourself, lash out at your family, and stop being open and intimate. Harmful feelings constrict your thoughts and you close yourself off from those around you. The emotions are trying express themselves, but you're not giving them an inch. You try to keep the lid on, but it's like a pressure cooker, boiling inside and ready to burst at any moment. As soon as you're triggered, it's a can of worms, exploding all over the place with flairs of rage, dismay, and doubt. When you let Internal Clutter stack up, it's going to come out sooner or later and then everyone loses.

As with External Clutter, there are three subclasses of Internal Clutter. Limiting Beliefs are unhealthy ways of thinking that prevent us from achieving our goals, Repressed Emotions are feelings from the past that have never gone away, and Self-Dislike is a sense of being uncomfortable when you're left alone to your thoughts.

Let's dive deeper into each of these classes of Internal Clutter.

Limiting Beliefs

The first type of Internal Clutter, Limiting Beliefs, are false ideas that keep you down. "I'll never be an organized person," is one example. These fabricated concepts might arise from your own self-doubts or they can be thrust upon you by what you're told. For example, if you grew up in a household where your parents always teased you, you might develop the Limiting Belief that you won't amount to anything. Gee thanks, Mom and Dad! Regardless of where these beliefs come from, the first step to battling them is to recognize they are lies.

Here's a Limiting Belief I held for a long time: if you let out your feelings, you'll never stop crying.

Turns out that's a lie I was telling myself. All emotions pass if you just allow yourself to feel them without judgment. I bottled my feelings away for years because I held this belief, and it led me to develop Repressed Emotions as a result.

How do you know whether a belief is limiting you or not? To identify Limiting Beliefs, start by concentrating on something you wish you had in your life. Maybe it's more friends. Or more time to spend with the friends you already have. Or more money. Or a promotion. Next, ask yourself why you don't already have the thing you want. Whatever excuses you come up with in your head in response to this question are Limiting Beliefs.

Fear

The second type of Internal Clutter, Fear, is a powerful emotion, and you've likely developed your own methods for coping with it. These aversions, ticks, and superstitions clutter your mind and your behavior. Pushing these fears to the backburner feels safe and avoids discomfort, but hinders your decluttering process. Fear is an emotion, and pressing emotions down is kind of like pumping up a Super Soaker. Sooner or later everything is going to come spewing out.

Don't fear your fear because when you make space for it, the feeling only lasts about 90 seconds. Better yet, you'll tap into the energy of the emotion and convert it into excitement. (I'll show you how to do this in Chapter 7.) But when you resist fear, it sticks around like a thorn in your side, poking you for attention. When emotions are left unadressed, they tend to linger, so we end up giving them more attention! It's a vicious cycle that leaves us exhausted. Then we wonder why we're depressed, tired, and distracted.

The trick to managing Fear is to let it come up naturally, accept it, and work with it. Otherwise, your mental space will become cluttered with unwanted fears that hang around like overstaying party guests.

Of course, you don't always have to let every emotion wash over you in every moment. Sometimes it's not appropriate to yell furiously, burst into tears, or scream with joy out of the blue. At a funeral, during a business meeting, during church, in the library, at the bank, and many other places we find ourselves, we can't let our emotions out of control. In these cases, put the emotion on pause, then find some time later in the day on your own to revisit the emotion and allow it to play out fully.

Repressed Trauma

The third and final type of Internal Clutter, Repressed Trauma, is a heavy experience that takes up a lot of space in your mind. It gets in the way of the decluttering process because it is scary to deal with, and ignoring it is so much easier. You are feeling this if you don't like being left alone with your thoughts. For many, this is why we distract ourselves with endless notifications and updates. If you are constantly 'busy' then you never have to be alone with your thoughts.

The problem is, when Internal Clutter as heavy as Repressed Trauma sits in your mind untouched for too long, you can begin to mistake it as part of your identity. When you let a haunting experience define who you are, you risk disliking yourself to the extent you dislike the memory.

In one eye-opening experiment subjects were asked to sit in a room for fifteen minutes and were given the option to either pass the time on their own or give themselves an electric shock. Even though the participants had said earlier that they would be willing to pay money to avoid being shocked, 67% of the male participants and 25% of the female participants decided to shock themselves during their alone time. They chose to feel physical pain rather than confront their Internal Clutter. Clearly, many of us have issues being alone with our thoughts. Many of my clients struggle with self-dislike and busy themselves to avoid facing their inner demons.

Recognize that Trauma is a form of injury, and often requires professional care to heal correctly. The exciting news is that when you are willing to deal with form of clutter, you'll realize that you possess extensive potential energy waiting to be tapped into. With external support and creative problem solving, you will grow a greater love for yourself and your community. When you practice loving yourself, you will feel happier in your skin. The self-dislike will dissipate like a dream upon waking.

External Clutter Mirrors Internal Clutter

Internal Clutter and External Clutter are closely linked, so when you experience clutter on one front, look for it on the other too. Living in a disheveled, unclean, or unsupportive environment can lead to physical and mental maladies. On the outside, you might gain extra weight or develop bad posture. On the inside, you might intensify feelings of anxiety or depression.

When I was a drug addict in my teenage years, I destroyed my body. Internally, I was repressing pain, which was reflected on the outside. I was as disorganized as ever and the clutter was appearing on my body too. I didn't respect myself and ended up with high cholesterol as a young, skinny girl among other health problems. But that changed when I removed the internal clutter and external clutter that was interfering with my life. I started to love myself more, I let the negativity pass, and I replaced my unhealthy environment with one in which I could thrive. The clutter disappeared.

In my most recent check-up, my doctor said I

have the liver of an infant, the kidneys of a teenager, and impossibly low cholesterol. No matter how cluttered you are on the inside or on the outside, it is completely reversible! When my mind was finally processing Internal Clutter in a healthy way, my body started processing External Clutter in a healthy way too. I began maintaining a healthy lifestyle inside and out. I haven't had the flu, felt Self-Dislike, administered an electric shock to myself, or had a cluttered inbox ever since.

Sounds Like A Lot...

You don't need to deal with a lifetime of Internal Clutter before you can clean up your basement or garage. But if you follow the steps laid out in this book, both types of clutter will go away in tandem, reflecting the good work you're doing on both fronts.

What's important is being able to sit with yourself and let negative feelings come and go naturally. Don't ignore them like a drawer full of junk. Notice you clutter and take gradual steps to work on it. It's not like you have to throw out all your old Pokémon cards by the end of the week.

Decluttering may mean scheduling a massage appointment for yourself on the calendar. It might mean getting out of a toxic relationship. Or it could be as simple as getting in the jacuzzi tonight. If you make more space for yourself in your life, you can utilize that space for self-improvement and decluttering. The more time you have, the more progress you can make, and it all starts with being present.

You don't have to dig into your problems, you don't even have to know what they are. You just have to be willing to make the space to let the magic happen.

Before we go any further, here's a quick note about how to make your way through this book: *full steam ahead*. Along the way, you might see interesting ideas and be tempted to put the book down and go start implementing bits and pieces of what I'm saying. But it's important to make it through the whole book.

This book is made to work as a complete system, and I kept it short for a reason. It's best to maintain your speed and make it through to the end. Then you can come back and start to apply things later on as you read it a second time.

If the captain of the Titanic would have followed this simple lesson, the ship's name perhaps wouldn't be synonymous with an embarrassing and tragic failure today. Optimistic historians believe the Titanic would not have sunk if it would have rammed the iceberg head-on rather than slowing down and hitting it sideways. In the final hours of April 14th, 1912, lookouts and bridgemen tried to warn Captain Edward J. Smith of the impending icefield ahead, but he ignored the warnings. It was First Officer William Murdoch who ordered a hard-a-starboard, a breakneck shift to the left, in an attempt to skirt by the unavoidable threat. This dramatic maneuver required Titanic personnel to reverse the engines and slow down the ship's momentum, sealing its fate. Without enough speed, the "water-proof" hull was breached in several places and the Titanic succumbed to the icy Atlantic.

If you lose steam and slow down halfway through the book, it will be difficult to guarantee any kind of success. Keep reading. Just one chapter a day until you're done.

Full. Steam. Ahead.

Chapter 2

How to Make Space

Have you ever worked hard to clear space in your garage, basement, or workshop and then watched in dismay as clutter reclaimed the area within a few days? Clutter has a way of growing back like weeds, and simply being knowledgeable about the differences between External Clutter and Internal Clutter isn't enough to stop the grow cycle. It's frustrating to make progress then lose it again. It can feel like one step forward and two steps back.

The problem is you can't make space on the outside until you first make space on the inside. That's why the clutter keeps coming back after you clear it away. External Clutter and Internal Clutter are linked and it's impossible to address one without the other. Those stacks of junk in the garage or the cabinets full of papers building up in the living room are symptoms of inner junk and build-up you can't ignore.

Getting rid of your External Clutter without addressing your Internal Clutter doesn't work. There is a reason why the majority of people who lose weight using programs like Weight Watchers (or on TV shows like The Biggest Loser) gain back every pound after they go off the diet. Body Clutter is external. That means if you have extra pounds on your hips it's a sign there is also emotional clutter within.

I struggled with the link between External and Internal Clutter during my teenage years. I was constantly moving between homes and leaving half my possessions behind, but every time I performed one of these purges, new clutter would rush in to fill the empty space. It felt like I'd chopped off one of the beast's heads only to see two new ones grow back in its place.

One of my clients had a similar problem. This

woman had a five-by-five section of her floor dedicated to shoeboxes of unorganized belongings. When I helped her go through what was in these boxes and created clear space on the floor where there had been none, it caused her so much anxiety she wouldn't speak to me for months. This begs the question, were the shoeboxes really the source of her clutter? Or was the apprehension she felt when seeing the empty floor space the true obstacle?

You might have picked up this book because you want to get rid of External Clutter, and I will definitely show you how to do that. But you also need to understand that External Clutter is a sign of Internal Clutter lurking below the surface. We cling to antiques, collectibles, heirlooms, memories, and other objects because we need them. We use them for a shield when there's something inside we aren't ready to confront.

Clining to the External

To protect ourselves from our negative emotions and destructive thoughts we cling to all three types of External Clutter as shields. For you, it might be Digital Clutter. Maybe you let constant notifications and an overflowing inbox keep you feeling busy. Or you might allow clutter into your life in the form of junk food, Netflix binges, and a sagging belly.

For me, it was drugs.

Growing up, I was the victim of emotional abuse, sexual abuse, and abandonment. Instead of dealing with my demons, I found solace in drugs. I was forced to attend AA when I was 13 years old. My brother committed suicide when I was 15. When I left the residential treatment center at age 17, I quickly spiraled back into my drug habits. By then my drug of choice was crack cocaine. It controlled my whole world. Crack was my clutter. It was the external expression of a deep internal pain I didn't want to confront head on.

And I clung to it, *hard.*

Crack is the epitome of addiction. When you smoke weed or take heavy psychedelics, the high might last a few hours. A single hit of heroin or crystal meth can satisfy you most of the day before you start to itch. But crack is a different animal.

Taking a hit of crack is the most blissful and amazing feeling in the world, unsurpassed by anything you've ever experienced. And then it starts to fade and you want another hit. Crack satisfies you for about ten seconds. My addicted friends and I could blow through $400 worth of cocaine each in about fifteen minutes. Crack wormed its way into every part of my life, like a virus. I clung to crack to avoid taking a hard look at my Internal Clutter. When all I could think about was the next dose, my emotional issues took a back seat.

Often when we seek to avoid inner discomfort, we use other things to keep us busy and distract us from our thoughts, pain, sadness, anger, and rage.

I was 15 years old when my brother took his life. I didn't know how to deal with his death in a healthy way. The feelings of rage, loss, and confusion were so intense I didn't want to let them in. So I distracted myself instead.

I would hop in the car with friends and drive an hour to pick up crack, then smoke it while driving another hour to pick up the next baggy. It was a non-stop lifestyle that I didn't want to escape. I was so desperate to cloak my Internal Clutter that I sold all of my brother's possessions for more crack. The harder I clung to the drug, the more cluttered my life became. Though I had few possessions I was cluttered with poor health, toxic relationships, and a cycle of addiction. I even married a crack addict at 19 so I could get away from my family and put up more walls between me and problems. I hardly batted an eye when my ex-husband burned his entire paycheck on crack every two weeks. At least I didn't have to face the music inside my head.

There were several occasions on which concerned neighbors, friends, or family members tried to intervene and send me to rehab, but I wasn't interested in getting clean because then I'd have to declutter my trauma. Even when I got off crack, I used a myriad of other drugs to maintain the illusion I wasn't in pain. I was homeless for five months, biking people around on pedicabs in San Diego for money, which I blew on drugs. I'd stay in roach motels or sleep in a friend's car. Even as I enrolled in meditation training and studied martial arts, I was on a cocktail of marijuana, ephedra, and painkillers.

One night I got pulled over for U-turning at a red light and police officers found crystal meth, scales, and plastic baggies. I was charged with possession and intent to sell. The judicial system gave me a choice: go to rehab or serve six years in prison. I opted for rehab. During my stint, though, all I could think about was getting out and getting high.

The itch I felt to fall back into drugs is the same itch my eventual client would feel when we removed her shoeboxes and cleared a 5x5 foot area on her basement floor. It's the same feeling those people on *Hoarders* experienced when the producers stripped away all of their stuff by force. It's a feeling of being exposed and naked. With no External Clutter to keep us safe, we have no protection from our Internal Clutter.

In Order to Push, We Cling

We cling to drugs, money, and stuff because it helps us push away something less tangible. Children hold onto their mother's legs on their first day of kindergarten because it soothes their fear of the unknown. Some of us obsess over food, porn, or exercise to dodge daily stressors like going home to a spouse we can't stand. Hoarders cling to External Clutter to mask their Internal Clutter. I had one client who was always buying new clothes to avoid doing laundry!

If you can't seem to keep your External Clutter at bay no matter how hard you try, it could be because you're running from Internal Clutter. But that's okay. You don't need to know why you're running. What's important is simply recognizing that you're hanging onto clutter. When you understand that clinging is an act of avoiding, the rest will figure itself out.

We might try desperately to protect ourselves from Internal Clutter by clinging to something external, but it's not a long term solution. In fact, it's a poor coping mechanism that only makes life harder in the long run.

My own Internal Clutter led to serious External Clutter, including homelessness, crime, and disrespecting my body. But I had no idea my unresolved trauma was the source of my issues at the time. Making the connection between outside and inside problems happened by accident.

I always knew I liked making order out of chaos. Orderly items like office supplies were one of the few possessions I lugged around from place to place. However, I didn't realize that making order within myself by beating drug addiction and facing my trauma is what would lead me to a more organized life.

The External Clutter Isn't Always Easy to See

While External Clutter is obvious sometimes, it can also be challenging to see. It isn't always a collection of objects, papers, or boxes. Some clutter shows up in our actions, and it can even appear to be healthy. For instance, someone might go to the gym way too much after a breakup to avoid addressing their internal feelings of rejection. Another may double down on work to keep herself focused on something else she sees as important. Even if you had all the immense love, support, and wealth you could imagine, Internal Clutter can still overwhelm you and it doesn't necessarily show up in an obvious way.

One of the most famous cases of invisible clutter is the tragic story of comedian Robin Williams. Williams played beloved characters in movies and television and had a special place in the hearts of millions around the world. Yet, he lived this "idyllic" life while masking a deep darkness inside. In 2014, Robin Williams was found in his hotel room, ruled death by suicide.

He fought deep problems inside for his whole life that nobody other than his loved ones knew about; the world took his incredible talent for granted. After his death, people found themselves asking, "How could this have happened to him?" Fans everywhere started to wonder what sort of Internal Clutter their friends and family might be hiding. A few brave individuals turned inward and searched themselves for pain they might have overlooked.

Williams dedicated his life to making others smile, and being there for others is a terrific trait, but if you stay busy to avoid your own insecurities, altruism can become another form of External Clutter. If mental illness could impact someone as iconic as Robin Williams, it could happen to anyone. No matter what form it takes, External Clutter is an indication that something is off on the inside.

Make Sure People are OK

Robin Williams' story is one example of how

external clutter can manifest itself in actions instead of items. His story underscores how devious clutter can be. No matter how well someone appears on the outside or how well they claim to be doing, we can never see what they're masking from us. The best way to be there for people is to check in on them, even if nothing seems to be wrong.

You don't want to be annoying, but it's important to check in with people. Many people tend to project an appearance that everything is fine because we don't want to admit we don't have it all figured out. But secretly we want to open up about our struggles and feel heard. When I was doing crack, I wished someone would reach out a helping hand. But I kept my guard up and pretended I didn't need anyone.

So how do you check in on the people you care about without being annoying? Here are a few strategies that have worked well for me:

- Writing letters
- Texting or calling just to check in
- Inviting people to get food or do other daily activities with you
- Asking how you can best be there for

someone
- Letting people know that you're always available as a resource
- If someone opens up to you, honor their trust and listen

When you check in with people, there are three main things to look out for. First, watch out for language like "busy," "crazy," "so much going on," and "whirlwind." A packed schedule is often a form of clutter that signals inner baggage. Second, listen when people refer to being "exhausted," "wiped out," "beat down," or "out of it." Running yourself until your tank is empty is another sign of running away from something emotional. Third, if you hear "he said," "she said," and other forms of drama, it's a symptom of inner turmoil. Distracting oneself by getting worked up about the actions of others isn't healthy.

Our clutter is often hidden from others, even disguising itself as positive. However, no matter how the clutter looks, it remains a problem for all people in whatever form it takes. Checking in with others, addressing any concerns you may have about their wellbeing, and making sure they know that their struggle is valid often means more to them than you can conceptualize. When people know they have support and aren't alone in their struggle, it's easier for them to begin the process of letting go.

Letting Go is Hard

Regardless of what your clutter looks like, it's impact can be monumental. Clutter often flies under the radar, its existence going unnoticed. It's easy to shove extra junk under the bed and into the attic so guests never come across it. You grasp tightly to the comfort our clutter provides, but with that sense of security comes a toxic dependence. Letting go is tough but necessary and worth the effort.

Often in life the things that are the hardest to let go of are also the things we most need to let go of. Whether our clutter comes in the form of extra weight on our bodies, extra things in our house, or extra responsibilities on our shoulders, we are weighed down by the things we want to protect ourselves with. We may kick and scream when these things are taken away but, like a toddler who wants a fifth lollipop, we will one day see that removing the clutter is for our own good.

One lady I worked with was attached to anything related to elephants and had a very hard time letting go of her elephant items. Elephant lamps, elephant pajamas, and elephant napkins were everywhere. In her house the elephants were on parade. Her family and friends fed her fetish by showering her in elephant accoutrements at every birthday and holiday because they knew she would cling to them with joy. However, the biggest elephant in the room was the fact that she had a serious problem with clutter.

She admitted to me that she was filling an elephant-shaped hole left behind from prior trauma. She never told me what the trauma was, and that's okay. It's not important how she experienced pain. I just knew I needed to help her let go.

But letting go was *hard.* I could tell because when she did get rid of an elephant vase, she wanted to make sure her prized possession went to the "right person" to take care of it. She was still clinging, even as she let go.

I worked with her on learning how to let go of

things in her life, forgiving herself, and recognizing her wonderful qualities. We cleared out the house, allowing the clinginess to withdraw at a gradual pace. Eventually she got rid of a sizable portion of her collection. The donations were only the beginning, however. We continued to work together, focusing on her Internal Clutter. When she saw she was strong enough to clean what was on the outside, she felt more empowered to face what was on the inside.

She didn't beat her elephant affinity and laundry apprehension at the same time. Letting go of her Internal Clutter didn't happen all at once. But once she was willing to show up for herself and let go, the rest took care of itself. If we have Exterior Clutter, be it elephants, porn addiction, gambling, or overeating, we're searching for protection from something we don't want to address. Letting go is scary and difficult, but it's worth it.

How can you tell whether your own collection signifies clutter or if it's just harmless fun? Ask yourself whether or not you could let it all go if need be. If the answer is no, you may want to revisit your motivation behind your collection.

Recently I worked with a client who had been clinging to Hopalong Cassidy memorabilia. It had been taking up space in his garage for almost 12 years. After a meeting with me, he became willing to let it all go and donated it to a local donation center, Habitat for Humanity. He had a healthy and detached relationship to the memorabilia.

When I was at my lowest during my crack addiction, I didn't see an ending. However, I had an encounter with the woman who became my mentor, and she helped me transition off the drugs. Her presence showed me there was more to life than the clutter I had built up to protect me from the weighty darkness in my mind. Letting go was a job in itself but I found myself in a much better place.

The Secret to Letting Go

Before you take care of others, you need to first make sure you are in a good place yourself. You can't pour from an empty cup. Once you're squared away, then you can properly give support to those who need it.

Help yourself first, don't distract yourself by clinging to Netflix, alcohol, or other family members who are going through their own pain. There's a common phrase stated during the safety lecture on airplanes: In the event that the cabin loses air pressure, secure your own oxygen mask before helping others. Airline stewards have to mention this life-saving tip because many people have the instinct to overlook their own safety in an effort to take care of those around them. Yet, when we do this, we are avoiding the fact that we could suffocate.

It turns out this was the answer for the woman who freaked out when I cleared a 5x5 foot space in her living room. She didn't call me for about a month. It was like aliens had abducted her. Those shoeboxes, it turns out, contained things she was holding onto for other people. She needed to learn to prioritize herself first in order to let it all go. But that wasn't easy. It was a process.

When we removed the boxes without addressing her Inner Clutter, it spooked her to see so much openness. It made her feel like she had to make a mess, like she had to put something there. It took her a few months to start putting herself first and clearing out her *Inner* boxes.

But facing down your Internal Clutter is so scary and difficult! What if you fail? The good news is there's no such thing as failure. As long as you can truly promise to put yourself first, you're on the right path. You can't mess this up. I'm going to lay out a simple set of practices you can follow to address your Internal Clutter, starting in the next chapter. You can do this.

I Promise You Can Do It

Nobody I have worked with has ever fully believed from the start that they were capable of facing down their Inner Clutter. Some believed it would be too much to bear, while others were certain it wouldn't be worth the effort. However, you are completely capable of turning around your life and leaving your External Clutter dependence behind. If I can let go of crack, the most addictive substance on the planet, you can let go of your clutter too.

My life's turnaround came after I was arrested. I was in my friend's car, pulled a U-turn at a red light, and was stopped by the police. The officers saw crystal meth and scales in my car and busted me on intent to distribute. The judicial system gave me a choice: rehab or six years of prison. I chose the one with fewer guards. I was kicked out of a few rehabilitation centers, but then I found the place that ended up being right for me.

My whole plan was sitting through rehab, then getting out and getting high again. However, after I was there for a few months, going to meetings, having a sponsor, and doing the work, I found something new inside myself: I wanted to try. I wanted to live. In 2004, I left the community as a role model, and I never touched crystal meth again.

We all have habits that prevent us from making progress with ourselves, but every obstacle can be overcome! I got sober in 2004, and started putting myself first after being in a codependent marriage in 2013. I'm telling you all this to show you the path is not linear, there are faults, but with the steps in this book you can arrive at a place where you can find happiness. It doesn't happen overnight, it's not a magic pill, it's not a quick fix, but the journey's worth it. And you can do it.

In the end, most of us want to hang on to the things we own. It's hard to let go. I'm not proud of how I sold my brother's things, but I won't lie, I'm happy I did. I don't need a memorial, I have my memories of him. After a while, everything I clung to was simply just extra, pulling me away from my own growth. When I was able to let it go was when my freedom began.

Without first addressing the Internal Clutter, you will not be able to address the External Clutter. Whether or not it's easy to see, External Clutter is often used to shield you from facing your Internal Clutter. As with Robin Williams, my elephant-loving client, and my own battle with crack addiction, External Clutter can distract you from your deep inner turbulence. The secret to letting go is to address the weight on your shoulders and check in with others to make sure they are alright. If I could beat crack, you can beat whatever you're going through too!

So how do you begin to address your Internal Clutter? Well, it's a three step process. First, you have to recognize and connect with the Divine Flow of Abundance. Next, you must practice Allowing the Now. Finally, you'll have to become a Happiness Seeking Missile. In the next chapter, we'll dive into Step 1 of the process...

Chapter 3

In and Out of the Flow

You've seen how dealing with your External Clutter needs to start from within or else the changes won't last. But let's be honest, confronting all of your internal garbage is terrifying. There's a ton of energy you've kept locked away and the thought of letting go can feel overwhelming. It can be scary to go deep. However, starting within is the key and this chapter will explain how to do it.

The first step in addressing your Internal Clutter is to understand and tap into the Divine Flow of Abundance. The 'Flow' is the energy in the universe, accessible to all of us, which helps us recognize and welcome blessings into our lives. It is what makes our lives better, and acceptance of it is the quickest way to clear up Internal Clutter. Even though it can be overwhelming, you have to be willing to relax and accept the Flow.

One great way to think about the Flow is like a car's headlights. When you wipe the headlights and turn your car on, they flare up like twin suns. You have access to the Flow, but your headlights are dirty and need a cleaning. Understanding this is the first step in freeing yourself. The Flow is the same power that created order out of chaos during the Big Bang, and the Flow can create order in your life too. When you clear out your Inner Clutter, the Flow starts to shine through. The more you clear, the brighter it will shine.

When your pipes get clogged through the accumulation of Internal Clutter, you're cut off from the Flow and lose energy and motivation. The astrophysicist Neil DeGrasse Tyson writes that we're made up of the four most common elements in the universe. We're stardust in human form, recognizing all the other amazing pieces of the universe around us. The Flow is the through-line between us and the greater mystery. When you are in tune with the Flow, you are living the highest form of yourself.

If the Flow is so good and it feels so crumby to block its shine out of our lives, then why do so many of us cling to our clutter? Is the Flow really hard to tap into? Why do we cut ourselves off?

Why We Cut Ourselves Off from the DFA

You've probably had the experience of feeling like circumstances are going your way and working out in your favor. When athletes experience this, you might say they are "In the zone," or "on fire." The same occurs in your personal life when you're having an amazing week and favors seem to be magically lining up for you. Think about the feeling when you win a raffle, or when you run across someone you love after a long time, or when you simply get recognized for doing a good job. That's the Divine Flow of Abundance in your life.

However, humans often tend to block the Flow from their lives. When something traumatic happens, many of us attempt to distance ourselves from the memories. We're more content with our trauma becoming ingrained than addressing our pain accordingly. In avoiding the pain, we push down true feelings, adding to our Internal Clutter and blocking the Flow.

Why do we allow blockage between us and the Flow? Negative experiences falsely color the way we perceive the world in relation to ourselves. We focus on the negatives and become attached to them. We lie to ourselves because it's hard to accept that we deserve the abundance of goodness that the world has to offer. Thus, we inadvertently shut ourselves off, retreating from all the goodness we deserve.

Opening back up to the Flow is challenging, even though doing so reintroduces goodness into your life. A lot of recognized power, even beneficial power, can seem overwhelming. Positive energy can feel especially intimidating if your environment has many inputs that condition you to think cynically of the world. However, after being reintroduced to the Flow, you'll see that it's like coming home. The Divine Flow never left you. In fact, it's been with you from the beginning.

We Can't Control Our Experiences

We have a connection to higher energy even before we're born. Babies come into the world with a completely clean slate, no blemishes on their souls. They do not have the rational capacity to avoid things that are uncomfortable or cling to the things that bring them joy. Babies are open to the Divine Flow and receive it fully.

Has anyone ever told you "Mozart makes babies smarter?" Whether you heard that from your mom, your friend, or the babysitter in *The Incredibles*, it's common knowledge that listening to classical music in the womb helps babies develop better cognitive impulses. What's additionally true is that taking care of your body during pregnancy will help your baby grow and thrive inside. Babies connect to mothers and share their nutrients as well as their hormone levels. If mom's in a stressful situation, the baby's probably not going to start out with the best connection to the Flow.

Science suggests we are connected to the Flow from birth. Genetics tie hand in hand with emotions. It's always been hard for me to slow down.

My parents were race car drivers, so going fast is in my blood. I'm sure you have similarities to your parents, too; similar interests or habitual mannerisms you can't explain. Maybe you and your father share a knack for photography. Perhaps your mother has a green thumb that you don't have but your brother does. All these blessings flow up and down the line, as do the negative experiences your family shares. Even in utero, the buildup of clutter begins.

You're not aware of the energy coming in until it's pointed out to you, and that's why you allow clutter to begin building up. It was only once I began yoga and mindfulness that I took a long look at my life. As children going through our lives, we don't make a conscious effort to repress things. We learn to allow our subconscious to defend us through clinging because we want to feel protected from negative emotions.

I'm a prime example of someone letting negative experiences disconnect me from the Flow. My life became so cluttered I couldn't see the point of living. The next section is my story. You'll see how I became more cluttered as I drew away from the Divine Flow, and how I found my way back.

Mel's Story

I went through many negative experiences as a child, and in response I was unknowingly cutting myself off from the Flow as a protective mechanism. Subsequently, these issues came bursting out of me when I least expected. I was one of those kids who threw a tantrum and hurled every toy from the box across the room. I broke windows. At five years old, I found a desire to start fires and explored this pyromania with vigor. I remember stealing money from my mother's purse to buy matches, building a rock circle, and lighting things on fire in the woods.

Where did my poor emotional coping skills come from? I watched my father lose his temper, smash plates on the ground, and break the timer on the stove, and that's where I learned how to express my emotions. I learned to deal with anger by breaking things whenever I felt powerless. On the other end of the scale, my mother resisted expressing her emotions. She held her cards close to the chest and refused to let anyone see. I took on my parents' negative coping strategies and became an unhealthy mix of their two toxic styles. I was cutting myself off from the Flow.

Our subconscious protects us and makes sure we feel safe from the world around us. If we perceive a threat, we do everything we can to keep it away. Unless we have perfectly healthy parents, healthy emotional coping isn't modeled for most of us. We allow clutter to build up and cut off our access to the Flow.

The first big block to my flow of energy was learning my grandfather had died. I was the one who got the phone call. I remember answering the phone and learning he'd died. Not long after that, my dad left. My parents split and he became my dad on Sundays only.

My mother and I moved around. We moved in with my mother's friend for a short period of time, and I experienced my first sexual trauma. When I was eight years old my mother left me to sleep in an RV with two older boys while she slept inside. The older boys assaulted me.

We finally got our own place and my mom had my older brother move in with us. He wasn't my mother's son, but my half-brother through my dad. We took him in. While he was with us, I had my second sexual trauma, this one coming at my brother's hands. This experience was added to the clutter.

The third sexual trauma came while we were living in the same place after my brother was kicked out. All three traumas happened while I was 8 years old. I found myself in a scary situation where an older stranger began messing with me in a parking lot. My mom's friend saw us and told my mom. When my mom confronted me, I was hysterical, and she slapped me across the face to get me to calm down. I took the trauma and added it to my clutter. I had a lot of Internal Clutter to deal with from a very early age.

In those traumatic moments, I learned it was bad to express my feelings. I believed I had to deal with everything on my own. I also learned my mom wasn't safe. I felt alone in the world. With all these negative realizations, the clutter kept building.

When I was 13, I went to juvie because I flipped out on my mom. I didn't hit her, but I started trashing the house and she called the cops on me. When they came, I lashed out at one, so he took me to the ground, handcuffed me, and escorted me out of the home. I was taken to juvenile detention and nobody fucked with me in there. I was 100lbs soaking wet, but I was crazy and unpredictable and people left me alone. The other girls could see how much Internal Clutter I had building up inside myself and how far away from the Flow I was, even if they couldn't put it into words.

At that point, there were many things blocking up my pipes. Abuse, neglect, and traumas ensured I wasn't calm in my own skin.

At 15, I ran away to live with my brother. He had stopped molesting me by then. Now he was 20, and I idolized him, even though he was messed up. One time, he asked "Did what I do to you affect you?" He was looking for answers, and I was honest. I told him the truth:

"Yes," I said, for the first time ever. My voice was shaking, but I felt it needed to be said. "What you did really affected me." After all those years of keeping my emotions bottled inside it felt good to finally let them out. The next day I found his body. He had committed suicide after I told him how his actions made me feel.

From my mom slapping me after I told her I'd been abused, I first learned to repress my emotions. Then when I finally got the courage to express myself to my brother, he took his own life. It felt like every time I tried to address my Internal Clutter there was another reason to stuff it down.

I was learning to block myself off from the Flow, one horrific experience at a time. The Divine Flow is what causes good things to happen and allows us to know we're healthy. Disconnected from the higher energy and boxed in with emotional clutter on my shoulders, I fell into a state of misery. My experience of the Flow didn't change until I developed a deeper level of awareness.

Becoming Aware is the Way We Begin to Heal

Healing comes through awareness of the Divine Flow. When your connection is blocked it keeps you from being your fullest self. Regardless of the means you choose to reconnect to the Flow, the act of attempting to reconnect is the first step in your healing process. Through recognition of the Flow and conscious effort, you begin to grow. With awareness you begin to take away from the Inner

Clutter and find your way back towards the Divine Flow of Abundance.

For me, the first glimmer of awareness happened in rehab when I read *The Miracle of Mindfulness*, by Thich Nhat Hanh. The book blew my mind wide open and I began soaking up books about a greater energy. Buddhism, Hinduism, Taoism, Islam, I read everything I could get my hands on. Through their teachings, I began to learn about the energy, the Divine Flow all around us. Finally, something began to chisel its way through the blockage within me.

I took this newly opened mind with me when I left rehab and saw the world in a different light. While life was still tough, there was a new appreciation in me for what there was to accomplish and experience. I began to put my mindfulness techniques into practice in the real world, working to clear the blockage within me. Over the years, these practices developed into the method I now use for myself and others to clear clutter in their lives, both Internal and External. I call the method Allowing the Now.

Allowing the Now

I use a simple practice called Allowing the Now. It's a way to clear your Internal Clutter and reconnect with the Divine Flow. Allowing the Now isn't about shutting down, pushing your emotions to the side, or pretending you're okay. Instead, it's a technique to make you aware of where you house your emotions. Through my time practicing Allowing the Now, I've learned I don't have to let my emotions wash over me, but I'm able to escort them to the waiting room and say "I'll get to you in a minute." I might do this when I have to work with a client or attend a meeting.

As you go throughout your day, you don't always have to allow every emotion to wash over you. That wouldn't be practical. But you can stay in touch with the emotions as they come up. Instead of shoving them down, show them to the waiting room and then find time later in the day to let them out and experience them fully. Feel your emotions deeply, but on your terms. You may not have control over the world, but you have control over yourself and you can choose to constantly grow for the better, reaching for the Flow.

As a result, you'll be much calmer and more energized. You can get more done in a day, focus on the tasks at hand, and end the day accomplished. You won't overwork, you'll take care of yourself, and you'll make regular deposits in your emotional bank account. When oxygen masks drop from above, you'll be able to take yours, breathe calmly, and then help others. You can acknowledge your feelings and let them in at their proper time.

I changed the way I dealt with emotional situations and decluttered my life, but it didn't happen automatically. When you learn and practice Allowing the Now, the key is to put in time with a conscious effort toward changing your life.

Making a Conscious Effort to Change

Why did I include a whole chapter on my addiction to crack in a book about cleaning up your house? Your outside life reflects how you feel on the inside. When you hire someone to clean or organize for you, the space is going to get dirty again. When you work on your Internal Clutter and reconnect with the Divine Flow, the feeling of accomplishment becomes normal. For you to achieve this goodness, you have to be willing to put in consistent effort to improve your life.

In order to lead a full and happy life, you have to be willing to shift and move, allowing yourself to change in the ebbs and flows. Being too rigid or set in your ways can lead to destruction. You need to surrender control and be flexible in order to make progress. It's tempting to clutch tightly, to make sure your life turns out the way you want it to. However, there's an old proverb: whatever bends does not break. If you stay too rigid, you will shatter underneath whatever comes your way.

No matter what you cling to in avoidance of your Internal Clutter, the walls can be broken down through recognition and conscious effort. Once I decided to begin addressing my traumas, my life changed for the better. I'm doing great now, and I'm at peace with my life. I attribute this to becoming aware of the Divine Flow and letting myself experience my life.

Now you know about the Divine Flow of Abundance. You've seen how you tend to distance yourself from the Flow, and how you thrive when you're connected to it. When you tear down the blockage of Internal Clutter, you're able to allow the energy to flow through you. The Flow is accessible to you, and you gain access to it through the technique of Allowing the Now.

Allowing the Now is the second step in addressing Internal Clutter. It's a simple, yet powerful tool you can use to change your life. In the next chapter, I'll show you exactly how to do it!

Chapter 4

Allowing the Now

You now understand how we block the Divine Flow from coming into our lives in order to shield ourselves from its awesome power. But understanding how this problem works isn't the same as knowing how to fix it. After all, most of us also understand that broccoli and kale are better food choices than donuts and ice cream. And we know it would be better to spend our free time at the library than at the mall. But we don't. The problem is we don't know how to get started. Change seems a long way off and we need a few simple strategies to follow.

When it comes to addressing your Internal

Clutter, there are two key strategies to implement. The first, called Allowing the Now, is covered in this chapter. Then, in the next chapter, I'll show you the second strategy of becoming a Happiness Seeking Missile. With that out of the way, the chapter after that will move from Internal Clutter to External Clutter. That's when I'll show you how to actually organize your junk drawers, cardboard boxes, and email inboxes.

Allowing the Now is a practice that takes just a few minutes per day. It will help you organize your inner junk pile and let the light in. Allowing the Now is the most important part of the decluttering process and you cannot skip this step.

Let me repeat that: *Don't skip this exercise, people!*

If you jump straight to organizing your outer world, the change won't last. The clutter will come right back. You have to declutter on the inside as well as the outside, and Allowing the Now is the most important tool for addressing your Internal Clutter. Let's start with a quick overview of how to do the exercise.

How to Allow the Now

Allowing the Now is an exercise to make you more aware of your internal and external environments. To do it, simply take a moment to slow down and be completely present. If you can sit and close your eyes that helps, but it's not required. All that matters is that you can be completely focused on the Now. That means don't do this exercise while you're driving or operating heavy machinery. You need to be able to take a deep breath, relax, and connect with yourself and the world around you.

Being present is hard because we humans are easily distracted. Many devices are designed to grab and hold onto your attention, and your phone is the primary culprit. Being present means accepting that you have autonomy to choose where you place your attention. Mindfully making that choice is an exercise, and like any exercise, you have to start small before building up the intensity.

When you first attempt Allowing the Now, your mind might be racing, and you might *think this is stupid*. That's okay. Your only job is to witness the Now and allow it. Notice how your mind races and wanders. When you realize that your mind is wandering, don't judge yourself. Just acknowledge that your mind was wandering and bring it back. It's okay. Remember, it's not called Resisting the Now. The key word is Allowing. Whatever happens is fine. Your mind might wander for the full five minutes, and that's still excellent progress! You can't do any wrong with this practice.

One tip that helps me is to focus on a physical feeling, such as placing your hand on your chest, or feeling your feet on the floor.

I've had some clients who were resistant to the practice of Allowing the Now. They made all kinds of excuses. One of the most common was, "I don't have time." But anyone can take part in Allowing the Now without taking any additional time out of the day. You can easily start Allowing the Now during other activities to save time.

For instance, we all have to go to the bathroom in the morning, right? Give yourself thirty seconds right there on the toilet to walk through Allowing the Now and dedicate yourself to being present and scanning your mind for clutter. If that grosses you out, do it in the shower instead of on the toilet. Lathering your hair is a perfect opportunity for

Allowing the Now. Or you can do it while you brush your teeth for two minutes each evening. "I don't have time" is no excuse when there are so many opportunities for Allowing the Now.

Outside of routines, you can be Allowing the Now during your downtime or "wasted" time. For example, if you're waiting in line at the grocery store and all you can think about is reaching the front of the line, you're not being present. You're anticipating a future event. You might get angry at the person in front of you when they take five minutes to find the right change for the cashier. You feel like your time is being wasted. However, that's only true if you allow that time to be a waste. You *could* use those five minutes of "wasted" time for Allowing the Now.

Waiting in line is one of those everyday situations that gets me frustrated because I hate feeling trapped. I've been stuck in a lot of negative places in my life, so when I feel like I can't move forward, it triggers a cascade of negative emotions. That's okay. I don't judge myself for being mad, I just accept it. I try to take advantage of these aggravating moments and use them to practice presence instead. Take 5 minutes in line at the store to check in, there's something better you could be doing with that time than fuming at the teenager in front of you, taking his sweet time to count out $63 in nickels.

Presence and internal space remove the frustration from your tedious shopping experience. Instead of feeling pent up and eager to push the other customer out of the way because you're in a hurry, you can create space to acknowledge your emotions and let them pass. Tell yourself, *I'm feeling frustrated because I have to wait. That's okay. I'm a human being and it's normal to get mad. And it will pass.* It won't stick around until dinnertime, you won't have to vent about it to your roommates, and you'll have less Internal Clutter to carry around as a result. You can still feel pissed off; you have every right to be! But reflection and acceptance will stop these emotions from affecting you for more than a few brief moments. Even shoulder to shoulder at the supermarket, you can create space on the inside for positive change.

Your Presence is Required

The secret to making all of this happen is a

dedication to being fully present. Shopping lines won't become spaces for positive change if you don't actively tune in to their value. It's just as easy to waste the 30 seconds in an elevator by pulling up your text messages as it is to invest that time in centering yourself and bringing your awareness to the present moment.

The Unfortunately Placed Towel

You might fail to be present every day during your most routine activities. In fact, it's during these habitual behaviors that you are most prone to zoning out. For instance, my mom keeps the kitchen towels draped on the fridge handle, a good five feet away from the sink. I always tell her to move the towels closer to the sink so she doesn't drip soapy water all over the floors and counters, but she won't listen. Drying her hands is not something she is present about, so she won't acknowledge that moving the towels closer to the sink will prevent clutter and improve her life.

Is the way she does it now messy and inefficient? I think so. Would it be better for my mom to have a more convenient place to drape her towels?

Not if she isn't present to the problem in the first place. Without presence, she's not making space in the kitchen for progress. If I moved the towels to a brand new spot right above the sink, they would end up back on the fridge again the next day.

The Unfinished Project

Another way presence can positively impact your life is when you bring more presence to your unfinished projects.

Craft-loving people often bury themselves in paint cans, modeling clay, and expensive fabrics for projects they'd love to do... someday. Car enthusiasts might sit on replacement parts for that dead Volkswagen in the garage and never get around to installing them. Serial gift-givers may not realize they are accumulating party favors faster than they can hand them out. In each case, people who lack presence sacrifice space for clutter.

If you have unfinished projects creating clutter and clogging your internal and external spaces, being present is the solution. Being present with a project means setting out to do what you aim to do and staying focused until it's completion. On the other hand, you may need to be present enough to realize which projects are truly a lost cause so you can toss them into the donation bin. Being present clears up the Internal Clutter associated with unfinished projects too, as it prevents you from ruminating on partially finished tasks.

Mindful Cleaning

Some of you motivated Type-A readers might have already noticed that it's possible to work on Internal Clutter and External Clutter at the same time by practicing Allowing the Now while you clean and declutter the house! Say hello to Mindful Cleaning. This is a powerful tool in your toolbox. You can simultaneously create space on the inside and the outside by staying fully present while you tidy up, but it's not easy.

For me, the first external space where I could be present with my actions and focus on building systems that worked for me to declutter was a yoga studio. When I transitioned from a messy kid to a passionate organizer in this studio, I didn't start by tidying up my personal External Clutter. I was still struggling with drug abuse, negative relationships, and physical clutter at home. But when I tidied up for others at the studio, I created a place for myself to be present and develop new decluttering strategies that were totally doable.

My yoga instructor and mentor gave me an amazing opportunity: I could have free range to use all equipment and courses at the center whenever I wanted in exchange for keeping the space clean. My job included vacuuming the floors, organizing the gear, and stocking vases with fresh flowers. I became a caretaker for the space and learned how to keep it clutter free while I enjoyed unlimited access to amazing resources.

I would vacuum the carpet in perfect lines, creating rows so identical and parallel it looked as if the carpet were installed that morning. It looked so good members and instructors would stop in their tracks when they saw the floors, afraid to step foot on the carpet and sully the flawlessness. My presence allowed me to turn the yoga center into an opportunity to work on my External Clutter management skills.

I couldn't sort out the clutter in my home environment as quickly as I did at the yoga studio, but being a caretaker did allow me to open up a little space for the magic to happen. When you're present, a little space is all you need to make progress. I went from someone who was chaotic, disorganized, and un-present to someone who loves creating order out of chaos. I caught my first glimmer of the Divine Flow of Energy coming into my life. When I had space to practice decluttering at the yoga studio, the blessings started flowing in.

Mastering the vacuum cleaner didn't take all that long, but creating a space where I could witness the benefits of decluttering took years because I didn't know how to be present. The key to letting go of clutter is making space and allowing the magic happen. You have to pay attention. You must commit to your self-improvement and happiness. You can vacuum the floor all day long, but that habit won't stick if you aren't engaged in the act of vacuuming, and appreciating how that act creates space for you to grow. No clean-up routine will work without the presence to acknowledge what works for you and what doesn't work for you. A lack of presence can cause the clutter to come back right after an intensive vacuuming session.

One Bite at a Time

Open up spaces for mindful presence one inch at a time. This approach is not about going on a deep dive into your worst clutter nightmares. I don't want a tidal wave of cardboard boxes or emotions to knock you down. This shouldn't be scary. Recognize that this is a gradual process. Mastery is the goal, and no one achieves mastery overnight.

In time, tiny changes add up to a complete lifestyle shift. For example, over the course of a few years, I went from being a hardcore carnivore to vegetarian, and then eventually vegan.

For most of my life I thought, *I'm never going vegetarian! I'm never going to give up meat!* But after a period of circumstantially not eating meat, something shifted inside of me. I noticed that I had more energy. Gradually, I added more changes to my diet. Sure enough, I had even more energy, and I found it easier to be mindfully present throughout the day.

I was literally decluttering my diet one bite at a time!

I cut more animal-based food, and added more plant-based food, and at some point along the way, I became fully vegetarian. I stayed vegetarian for two years before gradually shifting to veganism. I never thought this would happen! If you told Mel the Carnivore that someday she would become a vegan, she'd have told you where you could shove that fairy tale.

Bed, Bath, and the Abandoned Cart

When I started Allowing the Now and being present, I noticed a multitude of bad habits fading away. This wasn't restricted to just drug use.

I used to go to Bed, Bath, and Beyond and buy a bunch of stuff I didn't need. I can't explain it, I just loved wandering the aisles and fantasizing about having all sorts of *stuff* in my home. I bought items that in the back of my mind, I knew I would probably use only once, if at all. But for some reason, I had to have that second storage container.

With more mindfulness in my life, there was a gradual progression of this BB&B addiction fading away. First, I stopped stacking up my shopping cart, and would only buy the home items I thought I needed. After some time, I developed the habit of filling my cart with items I wanted, but then not buying them. I would leave my shopping cart in a random aisle for an employee to discover, and walk out of the store empty handed. Eventually I stopped going to BB&B altogether.

When you are mindfully present to a bad habit, one decision to rid the habit from your life sometimes isn't powerful enough to be lasting. It doesn't address the need you're trying to serve via the habit. When I was mindful of my BB&B obsession, I realized that what I needed to do was dream about my optimal environment at home. The store was great for fantasizing. It was only bad because I felt pressed to buy the goods I collected. By allowing myself to be present to my needs, I could stop the bad part of the habit. By being present, I was able to leave the clutter behind.

One, Easy, Everyday Practice

When you come home at the end of the day you're tired. You kick off your shoes, drop your jacket, slump your bag on the floor, and leave your lunch leftovers on the counter. As much as you don't want to deal with it right now, you're creating clutter like clockwork every time you walk inside.

Instead, try this: Put the shoes away in their proper place. Hang the jacket out of the way. Clean up your lunch, and hang up your work bag for your day tomorrow. You're doing yourself a favor by being present to your environment and making it an optimal space to get the rest you need. If you're extremely tired, the last thing you want is a pile of clutter giving you anxiety every time you glance in its direction.

When you practice presence, you start to spontaneously clean up your environment. Tidying your environment can actually be energizing. When you are mindfully present in your cleaning, it stops being a chore to dread and put off. It's as simple as walking from one room to the next and tossing one thing you don't need away.

These little, spontaneous improvements come from living in the present moment and they make a great impact over time. The best way to make a big splash with little actions is to be consistent about being present in your internal and external spaces.

The more acts of decluttering you do, the more you will realize how easy it is. The hard part is remaining present and doing it consistently.

My Struggle with Consistency

Consistency is more important than how long you spend vacuuming the floor. Don't get discouraged if you can't spend five minutes per day tuned into your internal space. If five minutes is too daunting, start with one minute per day so you can build a consistent habit. Do it while you shower. If you can do a minute of Allowing the Now every day, you'll be in better shape than if you practice Allowing the Now once per week for fifteen minutes.

You want to set yourself up to win, not to fail. Find what you *can* commit to and do it.

There was a period of time when I wasn't consistent with my mindfulness and it cost me. I practiced mindfulness and body awareness in yoga and martial arts, but after getting married I stopped practicing. For about 6 years I neglected to Allow the Now. I was not present.

This lack of consistency with my mindfulness practice kept me in a rut. My relationship was dysfunctional, and my drug abuse perpetuated. Like it or not, I had a routine, and I was consistently not present.

If I had been Allowing the Now every day, it wouldn't have taken me 12 years to get out of the relationship. I might have stopped abusing drugs much sooner. The daily practice of presence would have given me the space I needed to make changes, live my best life, and step into the Divine Flow of Abundance. It took me 6 years to remember to be present, and when I finally did, positive change was waiting right around the corner.

When I started checking in with myself again and practicing mindfulness consistently, I committed to my own happiness instead of my wife's. It was hard for me to let go of my relationship, but it was killing me to sacrifice my happiness. I was going down a bad road, one I was familiar with, and I had to make the choice to save myself. The trick was to prioritize my happiness by being present every day. I made that commitment back in 2012 and progress was immediate after that.

When I eventually left my wife, it was the most painful decision I ever made, but it was the most freeing. It was an intense accumulation of seven years of Allowing the Now, but it helped me realize that in order to be free to help others in my life, I had to declutter my life of my wife. I left with nothing but my office furniture, my Vitamix, and the juicer. That was all I could fit in my car.

For the first time in 12 years, I had room in my life. In that car stuffed with furniture, I was finally Allowing the Now and feeling the Divine Energy shining through my windshield. I was reminded of my need to be present, and I realized I needed help. I needed accountability. With my ex out of my life, I had room for someone who could provide me with coaching and accountability.

Consistency and Accountability

The trick to being consistent is to have accountability. This means having consistent external reminders to help you be present when you are most neglectful.

Motivation hack: Find someone to hold you accountable. Another human being will be far more impactful than an alarm on your phone. Dismissing phone alarms is too easy. Saying no, or admitting neglect, to a coach or accountability partner is more uncomfortable. Furthermore, sharing your consistency with them will be motivating and confidence building.

Accountability is one of my most important responsibilities to my clients. They check in with me every day and nobody wants to tell their coach they didn't take five minutes out of their day for Allowing the Now. Plus, if you're paying for a coach, you have skin in the game to be successful and not waste your time and money.

If you can't find a decluttering coach, at least find someone to be an accountability partner. It's similar to a gym partner. Not necessarily a close friend, but someone with whom you can build a relationship around accountability. Someone to make sure you don't skip your workout routine. Someone to encourage you, and you them.

Accountability drives consistency, and with consistency comes confidence and growth. And there's no shame in having someone help you, even for the easy tasks like Allowing the Now. You don't see athletes get to the professional level without coaches. People who are invested in you can push you further, faster. They see the value of the little details in your life, and the hindrances of your clutter, internal and external.

If you don't have a coach or an accountability partner, set an alarm for Allowing the Now on your phone that reminds you to be consistent every day. This can help you until you find another human being to help.

Without accountability, you'll just read this book and make no lasting changes. You must hold yourself accountable for your happiness, be consistent, and use a coach. When I did this, I finally gained the space I needed to let the magic happen and turn my life around for the better.

Conclusion

To practice Allowing the Now, the only requirement is your presence. You can practice presence at any time of any day in practically any place. When you perform this practice, you will open up internal and external space for progress. One step at a time, you can build the systems that work for you to declutter your life. If you're consistent about being present, the clutter will vanish in no time. To help stay on top of it, seek a coach or accountability partner and skyrocket your rate of progress to the next level.

While Allowing the Now will help you develop awareness of your negative thought patterns and other emotional baggage, it doesn't ensure change. That's why there is one step left for addressing your Internal Clutter. The Happiness Seeking Missile is an exercise to radically shift your inner dialogue and make you more positive. Master this and you'll be addressing your clutter before it even arises. In the next chapter I'll break it down...

Chapter 5

The Happiness Seeking Missile

Have you ever walked into a room, looked around, and immediately had your mind jump to the worst possible outcome? No matter the situation, negative thoughts have a way of creeping like unwelcome guests into your mind. It's frustrating to always be drawn to the negative, even when you try to focus on the good.

The problem is that changing your mindset to one of consistent positivity is a process. In every situation, there is a mixture of positive and negative influences. These influences factor into your perception of the world, with the negative ones tending to hold stronger sway in your mind.

Every day you are blanketed with messages promoting fear and conflict from the media. You need to do something proactive to counteract the negativity. While Allowing the Now can help you come to terms with trauma and emotional baggage, the activity you'll learn in this chapter, the Happiness Seeking Missile, can show you how to shape your perception of the world, becoming more positive and avoiding Internal Clutter before it even has a chance to grab a foothold.

The things you see and experience all shape your perspective. Repeated negative news can lead you to believe the world is a negative place, even when there is so much good happening.

You can clear out accumulated clutter all you want, but without an accompanying mindset shift you won't be able to properly process new information and keep the clutter from coming back. The best way to accomplish a positive mindset shift is with the Happiness Seeking Missile Technique. The Happiness Seeking Missile will allow you to recognize and appreciate goodness in the world around you. With proper practice, you can learn to see the good first and improve your mindset.

This may seem like a simple concept: looking for good makes you happier. However, the mind doesn't always do what you tell it to do. Keeping yourself focused on the positive is more difficult than it sounds. The Happiness Seeking Missile is a helpful tool to retrain your thought patterns to identify positivity and gratitude with greater ease.

How the Happiness Seeking Missile Works

The idea of the Happiness Seeking Missile is to bring conscious awareness to your outlook and shift toward a positive way of thinking. Across the media, there are many negatives to focus on. A thousand are dead in the Middle East. The climate crisis is overwhelming. Everyone is trapped in a financial rut. While these are all valid worries to have about the world, there's a whole other side of the coin that tends to go unnoticed.

Many good events happen every day, but we have trouble seeing them because our perspectives are trained to identify the negative. It's important to also see the good in the world.

Heat seeking missiles are used by the military in special operations. They have the unique ability to lock in on a heat signature and pursue their target until they detonate. Once a heat seeking missile is launched, it is 100% going to detonate on the hottest thing it can find. That's just what it does. It never gives up.

You can make a similar conscious decision to find something to be happy about every time you walk into a new room. Decide to launch a happiness missile every time you step through a doorway. Don't take no for an option. Find something to detonate your happiness on, regardless of how small or insignificant it might seem.

The Happiness Seeking Missile teaches you to look for the positives. Mr. Fred Rogers is an example of someone who embodied the Happiness Seeking Missile. Known worldwide for his show *Mr. Rogers' Neighborhood*, he strove to make others feel good, saying:

> *"When I was a boy and I would see scary things in the news, my mother would say to me 'look for the helpers. You will always find people that are helping.'"*

The comedian Jon Stewart echoed this sentiment with his comments around the September 11th terrorist attacks. Unlike many people who were shaken to the core, he found hope in the tragedy after watching so many heroes run into the collapsing buildings to save others whom they didn't know. Comedians received backlash for making jokes immediately following the tragedy, yet comics were desperate to get back on New York stages because they believed people needed to laugh more than ever.

At the Gotham Comedy Club in Manhattan the late Greg Giraldo joked about walking down the street after 9/11 and seeing a bachelorette party with rubber penises attached to their heads. Giraldo said mock-seriously that it was then he realized, "We're going to be OK. Life goes on."

However, positivity didn't make front page news for months following 9/11 because editors feared lighthearted stories would be deemed insensitive. Plus, negative headlines draw more eyes; they always have. Mourning is certainly an important experience, but is wallowing in sadness going to help anybody?

The Happiness Seeking Missile isn't about laughing in the face of tragedy but making uplifting observations even in times of despair. Latch onto the positive instead of the negative. Make joy your primary concern and sadness an afterthought. When you make joy and positivity the baseline in your life, before you know it, you'll reach a point where the negative dissipates.

Developing the Missile

I developed the Happiness Seeking Missile out of necessity, attempting to address negative influences in my own life. I was 35 and I was working at a furniture company where I oversaw multiple employees who weren't invested in their work. The main problem was our boss, who was simply one of the worst people I've ever met. He was narcissistic and often used tactics like yelling and intimidation to get what he wanted.

He also seemed to instinctively look for negatives and find ways to bring morale down. When the team wasn't performing well, he refused to accept that his own actions and choices were causing the trouble. Through his words, he began to drag us all down, creating a negative space in which it was hard to find happiness. After a while, I realized I could not emotionally survive in that position much longer. I needed positivity because the negativity was overwhelming. Given all the other challenges in my life, I was entertaining the idea of suicide.

So I made a choice. While there were plenty of reasons to stay negative, I ardently began to seek the positive. I searched desperately for what I loved and focused my energy on the good. The Happiness Seeking Missile grew out of this change in perspective.

Soon I was able to find joy in my job through the little things. I loved working with our designers on the phone. I loved the physical work of loading and unloading furniture. I loved getting deliveries done on time. Through this, I began to embody the Missile, seeing the positive in all the muck of negativity. I went from being suicidal to being able to appreciate where I was.

The experience taught me that all situations have the potential for positivity, no matter how bleak they seem. It's all about perspective.

Perspective?

We all bring a certain perspective to the world, like a lens on a camera. Your perspective determines what grabs your focus and what passes by unnoticed. Focusing on the positive is an exercise in changing your perspective.

There's a famous tale about a man who had to change his perspective. He walked into a Rabbi's office and said, "Rabbi, I don't know what to do. I have nine mouths to feed, my wife, her parents, and our kids. Our three dogs take up so much space. We live in a house that's too small without heat or electricity. I don't know what to do with my life."

The Rabbi thought for a moment then said, "Go to the market, buy a goat, and bring it into your home. Then come see me in a week."

The man jolted in his seat. "A goat, Rabbi? Are you sure?"

After seeing the Rabbi nod, the man sighed and left. A week later he came back.

"Rabbi," he said, "I don't know what your plan

is, but everything's even worse now! The goat eats all our clothes and poops everywhere. It hogs the food and the children are crying, my wife's sick of it, and the dogs won't stop howling. What can I do?"

"Get rid of the goat and come see me in a week."

The man nodded and left. A week later, he came bursting into the Rabbi's office. "Rabbi, I can't thank you enough! There's so much more room with that damn goat gone. It's quieter, cleaner, and everything smells better. I can't believe how fortunate we are!"

Buying the goat showed the man that happiness is all about perspective. The hardships in life are always easy to find. However, this mentality doesn't have to be a permanent feature. Becoming a Happiness Seeking Missile invites you to shift your perspective to the positive, to find the silver lining around the clouds.

When you look at the world in this new light, you'll notice things that make life worth living. I was suicidal when I developed the technique. Now, I'm happy to be here, and I'm actively trying to teach the Missile's lessons to anyone who will listen. Happiness is yours for the taking, but you have to reach out and grasp it.

How to do it

The work of the Happiness Seeking Missile comes from consistency. Don't think of this as a bandage over a wound. It's a process you can follow to clear the clutter within. While Allowing the Now will help you address Internal Clutter, the Missile will help you see the good around you. When you choose to look for happiness, your entire life will improve.

By cultivating positivity, you can have an incredible impact on your mind, body, and overall health. The more often you search for good and connect to the Divine Flow, the closer you'll get to the best version of yourself. The Missile will train you to constantly be on the lookout for the good in your life, even if you have to pull it from memory.

The first step is to establish a trigger, which acts as a reminder to launch a Happiness Seeking Missile. This is similar to how some people work on getting in shape by watching T.V. and doing push-ups during each commercial break. The break acts as a reminder to hit the deck. I like to use walking into a room as my trigger to launch a Happiness Seeking Missile.

There are two ways you can use this technique:

1. Recognize the Happy Things

Next time you walk into a room, identify one thing that brings you joy or makes you smile. Maybe you walk into a restaurant and see your friend who calls your name. Recognize that piece of joy. Maybe there's a robin's nest on the window. That's great to see. Recognizing the good is the most direct way of employing the Happiness Seeking Missile. Wherever you are, you can always find something to be happy about, no matter how small. You can approach any environment with an open mind and an optimistic outlook.

Being able to recognize happiness where you are is incredibly important. With all the negativity you absorb daily, it's easy to forget the good. When you walk into a room, sit in a park, play basketball, or do any other activity, apply this technique.

However, some days are a little harder than others. Some days everything seems terrible and it's difficult to recognize any happy thoughts. That's why there is a second method.

2. Three in the Chamber

Instead of detonating a Happiness Seeking Missile on something in the room around you, it's also possible to aim a missile inward. You can employ your own memories to create happy thoughts out of thin air. To load Three in the Chamber, get clear about three memories that bring you joy or make you feel good about your life. Train yourself to call any of them up if the need arises. With Three in the Chamber, you'll always have three awesome memories queued up in your mind, ready to bring a smile to your face. If you always have a few positive thoughts ready to go, they can serve as a steady base from which your happiness can grow.

This method revolves around seeking the good in every moment. You might be in a stressful situation and unable to concentrate on finding the good around you. With Three in the Chamber, you can reflect back on good memories and find calm.

Both of these techniques are active responses to a world that tends to drag you down. While life can feel overwhelming, you can launch a Happiness Seeking Missile at something in the room around you or you can detonate one inward.

The Missile Shows Truth

It is possible to find good in all situations. Shifting your focus can help you withstand negativity. When I was working at the furniture store with my terrible boss, I survived because I sought out the positive. I started launching Happiness Seeking Missiles.

However, that doesn't make it okay that my boss created such a negative environment. I appreciated the positives, but I eventually had the presence to leave that position. I saw I could find some other place without the negativity. Don't use the Missile to stay in a toxic environment without standing up for yourself, but use it as a stepping stone to get to a better place.

The missile will train you to appreciate the good and to differentiate between the good and the bad. When you habitually seek happiness, you'll gain the strength to leave tough situations.

You Can't Bring Everyone with You

Healing is a process. The first step is recognizing you have to make a change. The second is recognizing the change will not be immediate. The third step is understanding you won't be able to bring everyone along with you. Some people choose to turn away from happiness.

It can be easy to buy into negative news and forget that happiness exists in the world around us. Use the Missile to constantly keep yourself on the lookout for good.

I tell my clients a story about two boys who fell from a tree, broke their legs and were taken to the hospital by strangers. The first boy looked at the situation and his face fell.

"My parents weren't here to help me," he said, "I wish they were."

The second boy looked over at him and smiled. "But we're going to the hospital and a group of kind people came to help us."

This is the core of the Happiness Seeking Missile: Attempt to find happiness in every situation. These boys were in the same scenario, but one chose negativity while the other chose positivity. Learn to approach all situations in similar fashion. Everything happens for a reason and the Missile can help you find the good everywhere.

As you move forward, ask yourself how you want to live. You don't get to choose the situations that come your way, but you are in charge of how you react. Develop the Happiness Seeking Missile and make sure to load Three in the Chamber. These are practices that will lead to a better life filled with gratitude, appreciation, and peace. It's your choice.

Up to this point, we've talked about the importance of addressing what's on the inside. However, in the next chapter, we'll get into the nitty-gritty of decluttering. It's time to clean a room...

Chapter 6

Organize Any Space

Up to this point, you've learned about the two main kinds of clutter, Internal and External, what causes them, and how to recognize them. You've also seen how to address your Internal Clutter by unblocking the Flow, Allowing the Now, and launching a few Happiness Seeking Missiles. The next step is to deal with the External Clutter. In this chapter I'll show you a simple approach to purge both Physical and Digital Clutter from your life.

Physical Clutter is composed of objects and items that you cling to for protection from your Inner Clutter. As you begin to clean up your External Clutter stay patient and approach your items with a healthy mindset. Don't hold onto something for fear of not being able to get it again.

Digital Clutter is composed of files, PDFs, photos, games, messages, notifications, and documents. It's just as important to keep the digital side of your life clean as it is to clear out the physical side. At the end of the chapter, I'll show you how to do it.

It's normal to feel anxious when it comes to tackling your External Clutter. Decluttering means going through everything from yesterday's trash to decades worth of accumulated memories, and that can be stressful. Underneath this anxiety is fear. Decluttering makes you anxious because you are afraid to make the wrong decision and regret getting rid of something.

However, when you approach this process with the right mindset, it's easy. Giving this process time and attention is important. Don't rush through this. Failing to give each item adequate attention can cause confusion and fatigue. Approach every item with the intent of figuring out whether it still holds value. Clean with patience and respect for your items. There is a logical and peaceful progression you can follow to declutter your stuff without fear. It requires seven steps.

The Seven Steps to Organize Any Space

Clutter can be intimidating. It builds up over a long period of time and you often fail to realize how large it has become until clean-up time. When you think about tackling your most cluttered spaces you might have thoughts like "Where do I even start?" It's okay to be nervous because I'm going to break down all your worries!

The biggest key to success is to start small. There's no need to tackle everything at once. You will gradually address each item over the course of seven steps. You won't make a mistake in what you decide to keep and get rid of. Completing each of the steps will build your confidence for the next pass, as this is an ongoing process. The Seven Steps are a big project but you're more than capable of handling it! The first step is...

1. Preparation

When it comes to clearing out the clutter, some people tend to throw themselves headlong into the task, hoping to finish the job as quickly as possible. However, what's most effective is to slow down and work out a good strategy before you rush in. If you aren't ready to start, you won't be able to maintain the Seven Steps for the long haul.

When you're cleaning the desk, you may come across a pen that's worthless to someone else, but was the pen your grandfather gave you before he passed away. You don't want to have a cluttered mind and get rid of that one! Make sure you give this process the attention it deserves, as this is not a time for rushed decisions.

Being present will allow you to make the right decisions during the decluttering. Before you begin the actual cleaning process, find a comfortable place and sit for five minutes. Take the time to check in with yourself and practice Allowing the Now. Find your center. Let the emotions flow into you, through you, and out again. Feel your feet against the floor, how sturdy you are, and how much strength there is in your body.

With your eyes closed notice what's around you. What can you smell, hear, taste, and touch? Set a timer with a gentle alarm to go off in five minutes. Until then, this is your space and it's okay to be yourself here.

Before you begin cleaning, make sure you have all the necessary materials: trash and recycle containers, towels, wipes, polish, and anything that helps make an area look brand new.

Establish three containers for trash, recycling, and donations. This way you can sort things easily. Throw away anything that is obviously useless. Recycle anything made of paper or plastic. Donate anything someone else may need.

Additionally, make sure your cleaning supplies are always on hand so the things you choose to place in the keep pile will be returned to a clean environment. If you don't clean things as you go, your newly uncluttered spaces will invite clutter to gather again.

Once you're present through Allowing the Now, work from this mindful place. Choose an area to work on. Be sure to find a space that is manageable. You don't want to go through the whole house at once. Focus on one bag, box, drawer of junk, or square foot at a time. Small steps can lead to big results.

While these seven steps are all easy, the process takes time. Decluttering can cause intense emotions and you have to take it easy. You can become emotional around items that hold meaning to you or remind you of significant people or events. Be kind to yourself in these moments. Don't get overwhelmed. Breathe and stay calm. Then proceed to Step 2...

2. Like with Like

The second step is to take everything out of the drawer, box, or corner you have chosen to declutter one item at a time. Sort items into general categories first, and you can do a deeper sort after. Gather office supplies in one pile, books in another, and papers in a third. It's important to take the items out one at a time as you put them into your piles. Dumping everything out just transfers the problem to a new space. Place your articles carefully and don't make a further mess. The most important part about this step is to avoid jumping to any decisions. That's when you wind up feeling overwhelmed by trying to make two decisions at once. Sorting is one process and decision making is another.

Sorting forces you to consider each item. Grouping the items together helps you quickly compare each new pen you find with every other pen you own. Is this really the one you need to keep? Why is this one so special?

When you see a pen by itself, it's easy to justify keeping it around. It's a pen, after all, it's useful. That may be true, but you have many other useful pens. Grouping the items puts them in context and allows you to see the bigger picture.

The second purpose of this step is to keep your decluttering orderly and systematic. You can even leave halfway through and the piles will be waiting for you when you return. Once you have everything organized, it's time for a...

3. Fresh Start

After you've sorted your clutter into piles, take a moment and use those cleaning products to scrub down the space you removed the objects from. You should have a spotless drawer, box, desktop, or attic corner. Don't miss an inch. Clean the space thoroughly and then take a break.

The reason to take a step back, clean, and rest here during Step 3 is because the fourth step is the tough one: Decision Time. In this step, you're going to begin choosing what you want to do with each item. Before you dive into that, it's important to make sure you're mentally prepared.

For a moment, take your mind off the task ahead of you. Celebrate the progress you've already made. You're doing great! Don't rush through the process. Everything will have its place soon enough. Take a few deep breaths and enjoy the clear space you created. Then, when you're ready, it's...

4. Decision Time

For many people, this is the most challenging step. But you're ready for this. This clutter has been taking up space in your life for far too long. It's time to make decisions about what's going and what's worth keeping.

Survey your piles. There are two ways to go about this. First, you can simply move from the smallest pile to the largest. I like this method because you get to warm up on the smaller piles in preparation for the larger ones down the line. The other way of doing it is by choosing the category that's the easiest for you to make decisions about. Which category will give you the most trouble? Which would be a breeze? Choose the one that's a breeze and go for it.

Every item deserves your consideration. Pick up one item, look at it, think of the times you've had with it and what you used it for. If you have twenty pens, do you really need the 21st? Make sure you give every item time and recognition before your decision. Even if you keep 99% of your items during this session of decluttering, focus on the 1% you chose to give away!

In my experience, I have noticed that people will get rid of 30-60% of their items without even trying! While this method is not the fastest way of decluttering, it's the most thorough and cognizant. With this approach, you give yourself time to fully digest every item. Your decisions aren't rushed or pressured, they're made by you and you alone. You have more than enough time to focus on making the right choice.

If something's hard to get rid of, that's okay, put it in the keep pile. This process isn't a one-time thing, it's an ongoing conversation with yourself about what matters to you in various stages of your life. You can do this multiple times until you're finally decluttered. Your tastes will grow and change as you do.

Through this step, focus on the wins, the stuff you let go of. It doesn't matter what you keep for the next round, all that matters are the successes, what you are able to let go of. Think of it as building the "letting go" muscle. Every time you let go of something, you're strengthening it. You don't go to the gym and lift weights only once to get results right? Don't focus on what you didn't do, but what you did. When this step is over, you're...

5. Homeward Bound

This step is when you'll put everything away. In order to not recreate the clutter from before, keep your piles together. Start with whatever already has a home first, and then group similar items together.

Be present with each item and put it where it feels right. When the items have pre-determined places, there's less of a mess. Then move on to the items you're not sure of. Remember, *Like with Like* when putting things away. Keep like items with other like items.

When addressing larger items, think about how often you use them. Things like Christmas lights are only needed once per year so they can go in a less accessible space than a barbeque fork. Necessity dictates where things should go.

Also during this step, take the time to appreciate what you just did. You lifted a big emotional weight from your shoulders with those decisions. Be present with your emotions, forgive and congratulate yourself for your hard work. That leads to...

6. Tying Up the Loose Ends

It's time to take the clutter away! Bag the trash, take it to the can and dump it. Do the same thing with recycling. Don't throw the donation bags in the garage, take them immediately!

Leaving the donations until later is like leaving a child alone with a marshmallow, it's too tempting to resist. You don't want to end up donating these items back to yourself! You may feel the urge to go through the pile and second-guess yourself. Don't give yourself the chance. Toss or donate the possessions you're removing from your house right away.

Also, don't try to give your stuff away to other people. While you might think your friend will love a certain shirt or photo, you don't know for sure. Don't pressure other people to take your stuff. Give them the option and let them know you are getting rid of it if they don't come and get it before a certain date. Then follow through and take the stuff away if they don't grab it.

Undoubtedly there will be certain pieces you don't know what to do with, especially on your first pass. Don't panic. There's a simple solution involving a box, your calendar, and a very deep closet. Take all those things, put them in the box, put a date on the box, shove it into the closet, and set a reminder to open that box in six months. You'll come at those articles with a fresh perspective. Then repeat this process as many times as is necessary.

7. Form the Habit

The key to this technique is consistency. After you go through this process, you'll be more comfortable cleaning out the clutter in your life. With practice, you will be able to go through the piles with more confidence every time. You'll be stunned at how much space your life will suddenly have!

Some of my clients require years of nudging to even begin this process. Others jump right in and the only way I can help is to fill my truck up with their donations and shuttle them to the donation center. Treat decluttering as seriously as going to the doctor; cleaning this mess is for your mental health overall. If something comes up, don't brush it off, reschedule and make up the time later.

These steps are a solution for the accumulated items in your life. This process takes your attention and deserves your respect. In the end, if you follow these steps you will be more satisfied with your decisions than if you would have hastily gathered up a group of things to throw away. This way you can be confident you're making the right decision.

During this process, you will come across some

things you'll have trouble getting rid of. Maybe you'll find a corsage from your prom, a picture of you and your college friends having a beer on the dock, or a macaroni picture made by your little Rembrandt in first grade. These kinds of sentimental items bring back so many wonderful memories. How could you get rid of them?

The answer is you already have. If you haven't taken something out for years, then you've already gotten rid of it. You might have wonderful memories of these items and they might bring you back to that place, but they aren't hung on a wall for you to see every day. You don't need the object itself in order to enjoy the memories. You can let the object go.

Tips and Tricks

Everything in this world gives off an energy that's strongest when used to its fullest potential. When you box up items, you're sealing away their energy. You are acknowledging they no longer have a real use in your life. This means it's okay to let them go.

On an individual level, you can use the objects

you find as inspiration before ultimately tossing or donating them. The corsage from your prom is a dried flower, not a portal back to your high school years. Scan the photo of your college friends and send it to them as a way to reconnect. You don't need to keep your child's first grade art project to prove your love. You are strong enough to recognize these items for their worth and get rid of them if they do not fit into your life anymore.

This is a taxing process, but there are always solutions. Your old college shirts have value, even if they're not being worn. Collect them up and sew them into a blanket. If your books are taking up space but you don't want to throw them away, donate them to the local library. Everything you box away is not being used to its fullest purpose.

There are some items you might be tempted to hold on to because of their value in the future. I would caution against this. Your comic book collection is most likely only worth anything to you. Additionally, you'll have to go through the hassle of selling it all. Instead, I recommend donating these pieces. You will be able to receive the full value for the items as a tax write off! (Check with your accountant first of course)

As you go through your cluttered spaces, you'll begin to see all the memories that have accumulated over the years. Parse these items, decide which to keep, then let go of the rest.

Deleting Digital Clutter

Digital Clutter is just as much a problem as the things that fill our lives off the screen. Although some may not consider anything saved online to be clutter, this is another area of our lives we must keep ordered! In the digital world it's easy to let things accumulate. We put things in different folders, thinking, "I'll get to it later," or we allow emails to pile up in our inboxes. All these forms of Digital Clutter take up our storage space and put stress upon our shoulders.

To solve this problem, people all across the world have taken it upon themselves to begin cleaning up the digital mess. With many available online resources, there are plenty of ways to start letting go of your e-junk.

While Physical Clutter takes up space, which is limited, its digital counterpart has unlimited storage to contend with, as long as you're willing to pay for it. It's fantastic to take advantage of programs that organize your photos and save your files. But don't fall into the trap of relying on these clouds to hold your memories instead of working to make sure you're not clutching onto anything extra.

When it comes to tackling thousands of emails, you have to decide which are important, and how to accommodate new ones coming in every day. Some programs allow you to designate emails to remove from your inbox automatically. Other services package all the spam you receive every 24 hours and deliver the entire bundle in a single message every morning. However you decide to go about sorting your email, know that there are many different ways to clean the clutter!

Files are different from emails. Mixed into your hard drive are photos of loved ones, jokes, important forms, PDFs from college, personal writing, and a huge array of random files. When you go to address this clutter, you have to ask yourself what's worth keeping and what's worth moving to the trash.

One key to working through Digital Clutter

is organization. Folders and subfolders are great ways to keep track of everything and organize your electronic life. There are also online services that can store your files if you want to clear off your desktop. You don't need to get rid of it all, but you do need to have a strong system you'll be able to stick to!

Digital Clutter can seem impossible to sift through but it's entirely possible. You just need to designate enough time for a thorough purge! Make sure you don't throw out the important bills. Move files to the trash and empty it. Digital Clutter is just like the rest, you are completely capable of handling the mess.

Conclusion

Cleaning up your clutter can be a difficult task. Doubt can creep into your mind and make you reconsider getting rid of certain things. It's easy to be nervous about making the wrong decisions.

You are perfectly capable of cleaning up the clutter in your life. Take a step back and approach the process with organization and presence and you will make the proper decisions. When you group the items and consider them one at a time, it's much easier to make the correct decision about what you want to do with each one.

Now that we know how to handle the clutter on the outside, let's talk about how to organize your Internal Clutter...

Chapter 7

Organized on the Inside

Now that you understand how to organize your External Clutter, it's time to talk about bringing order to your Inner Clutter too. If you don't address the Internal Clutter, the External Clutter will keep coming back. External Clutter is a visual representation of Inner Clutter. If you have extra pounds on your body, or boxes stacked up in your attic, these are symptoms of inner turmoil. When you allow Internal Clutter to build up, you block yourself off from the Divine Flow of Abundance and limit the energy level in your life. The longer you wait to clear out the clutter, the more blockage builds up between you and the Flow. Addressing your Internal Clutter is as important, if not more so, than addressing your External Clutter.

No matter how intimidating it may seem, Internal Clutter is not something you can avoid. In this chapter I'll show you how to start sifting through your inner junk and organizing it, just like you did with your physical and digital stuff in the last chapter. Specifically, I'll walk through some strategies for how to handle the three major types of Internal Clutter: Limiting Beliefs, Fears, and Repressed Trauma. By examining and organizing these three categories of Internal Clutter, you can become more free.

While Internal Clutter may seem like a giant barrier to your happiness, it can be broken apart with consistent practice. Let's begin with the first type of Internal Clutter…

Limiting Beliefs

Your beliefs define you. They guide your relationships, passions, and motivations. However, your beliefs also limit you and hold you back. You might believe you can't do something or you're not good enough. These are negative beliefs that don't serve you.

There are two main places where Limiting Beliefs originate: emotions and experiences.

Emotion

The first source of Limiting Beliefs is emotion. Many beliefs are formed based on strong feelings. Thus, emotions have a large impact on how you see the world and think about it. Strong positive emotions can create empowering beliefs that help you reach your best self, while negative emotions can create Limiting Beliefs that drive you to your worst.

It can be tempting to ignore bad feelings, saying phrases such as, "Oh no, I'm fine," instead of confronting your issues. However, emotions are meant to be felt and experienced, both the positive and the negative. Denying some feelings or wallowing in others is harmful and can reinforce Limiting Beliefs. In order to dispel Limiting Beliefs, you must reframe your narrative about your feelings. This is the way to tear down your Internal Clutter.

When emotions arise naturally, allow them to come up. It's not healthy to deny your feelings. Believing you shouldn't be feeling happy during a funeral or sad at Disneyland can lead you to repress your true feelings. This repression leads to Limiting Beliefs and confusion. Limiting Beliefs make it difficult to clear away your Inner Clutter.

Dwelling on repressed feelings only brings about pain and a false sense of self. What matters are your emotions in the present moment. How you interact with these emotions determines how much Inner Clutter you will have to work against. When you experience emotions in a healthy way, you're building your personality for the better.

In order to address your Limiting Beliefs, you must come to terms with your feelings. However, before you do that, there is a second source of Limiting Beliefs to talk about...

Experiences

The second way for Limiting Beliefs to develop is through your life experiences. Like emotions, experiences aren't inherently good or bad. Positive experiences like being praised on an art project can be terrific sources of comfort for you. Negative experiences, on the other hand, have the potential to perpetuate beliefs about yourself. This is another way Limiting Beliefs develop, adding on to your Internal Clutter. Take me, for example.

When I was a child, I was abandoned many times, as I saw my parents, siblings, and friends all leave my life. Through my experiences, I developed the belief that all people would eventually leave me. My reaction to this was to push others away and keep them out of my life as much as I could so they wouldn't have the chance to hurt me. Even though this belief was false, it caused me to have an outsized reaction.

Your experiences impact your beliefs which, in turn, impact your life. I experienced people leaving my life, so I believed everyone would leave, leading me to push others away. When I truly examined my experiences, though, I saw I was only focusing on those who left rather than everyone else who stayed. There was so much good surrounding me, but my beliefs were rooted in negative experiences and made me think I was unworthy of happiness.

Together

Your emotions and experiences work together to dictate your beliefs. If you develop Limiting Beliefs, they will add to your Inner Clutter. Your beliefs influence everything from how you'll do on a test to whether or not your friends will like you. If you don't address your Limiting Beliefs, you won't be able to fully live your best life.

Only you can know how to declutter your own Limited Beliefs. However, you absolutely *can* do it. With a little work, you will be able to have a much better life, free from Internal Clutter.

How to Dispel Limiting Beliefs

When you allow Limiting Beliefs to creep in, false narratives about who you are can rear their ugly heads. When the mind is sick, the body will suffer. It's your responsibility to own your well-being and take care of your mind. Let's talk about how to dispel Limiting Beliefs.

You have all the tools you need to begin dismantling your Limiting Beliefs! The strategies you learned in the previous chapters, Allowing the Now and the Happiness Seeking Missile, are the main tools for addressing Internal Clutter. Allowing the Now teaches you to recognize and welcome your emotions. The Happiness Seeking Missile shows you how to ensure all new experiences you have are positive. Now I'm going to show you how to use these familiar methods, along with a few new techniques, to break down your Limiting Beliefs...

1. Recognizing Emotions

The first step in dismissing your Limiting Beliefs is to take a deep breath and employ Allowing the Now. Greet your thoughts and emotions at the door. Let every emotion in, recognize it, then allow it to pass on its way. Your subconscious is your friend, it will never give you more than you can emotionally address at the time.

There are two options for handling emotions: acknowledge them and begin working with them or press them down until they explode out like carbonation under a cork. Acknowledgment will help you identify your emotions so you can gain power over your Limiting Beliefs. When you can recognize your emotions, you'll be able to address them properly.

2. Recognizing Limiting Beliefs

Limiting Beliefs vary and yours are not necessarily the same as your neighbor's. Therefore, the second step in this process is to figure out what your personal Limiting Beliefs are. Take a look at your life. What are you telling yourself you're unable to do?

Limiting Beliefs manifest themselves differently in each of us depending on life experiences.

- "I can't play golf because golf is a rich man's game and I won't belong since I don't make enough money."
- "I can never ask her on a date, she'll for sure say no."
- "I'm just a crack addict and I can't be anything more."

In the middle of the word "belief" is "lie." Your Limiting Beliefs only exist because of your emotions and experiences, not because they're true.

You are capable of wonderful things, regardless of what your mind says.

In 2007, the NBA player Shaun Livingstone dislocated his left knee cap, broke his left leg, and tore his meniscus, ACL, and MCL on the same play. After this devastating injury, nobody would have blamed Livingstone for retiring. However, he overcame the adversity, both internal and external, and came back to win two championships. Once you recognize your Limiting Beliefs, you'll be able to take care of them accordingly. You can allow your Limiting Beliefs to hold you back or you can choose to overcome them.

3. The List of New Beliefs

Here's an exercise to help you identify your Limiting Beliefs and decide which ones to focus on first. All you need is a piece of paper, a pen, an open mind, and some space to yourself for thoughtful reflection.

- Fold the paper in half. On one half, write down every Limiting Belief you can think of. Allow yourself to feel these things, and don't judge your beliefs or feelings as wrong or inappropriate. There's no need to rush, everything will come in its time.

- Take a moment to think about how these beliefs have shaped your life. There's a lesson in everything, and this practice is no exception. Take a moment to tell the feelings they don't have a hold on you anymore.
- Now, unfold the paper. Across from the negative beliefs, write new beliefs that contradict the old ones. Then, like an actor rehearsing lines, read these new beliefs out loud to your little you inside, your subconscious mind. Give little you a name. Mine's named after my niece. Whenever I say these beliefs, mentally or verbally, I imagine saying them to her. Whenever I say or think any belief, I ask myself "Is this something I'd want to teach her? If I wouldn't tell her this, why am I telling myself?"
- Put the paper away in a place where you won't lose it (mine's in my wallet). Going forward, if a negative belief comes up, turn to your little you, look them in the imaginary eyes, say "cancel, cancel," and then repeat the new belief.
- The final step is consistency. Repeat and learn these new beliefs. When the old

thoughts come creeping back in, treat them like unwelcomed solicitors at your door and get rid of them!

- Repeat the new beliefs to yourself and your audience. Refuse to let the old beliefs dominate you. Remind yourself repeatedly, as many times as it takes, to condition these new beliefs into your mind. You deserve to be here and to be happy.

When I implemented this practice and took my Limiting Beliefs head on, I saw a rapid change in my mindset.

- "I'm not worthy" became "I'm good enough."
- "People will abandon me" became "people come and go, and their decisions are not a reflection upon me as a person."
- "I can't ask her out" became "I can be honest about my feelings to others, and how they respond is out of my control."

You may think you're "just messy" and can't change your slovenly ways. That's a Limiting Belief! Prove yourself wrong. By recognizing and addressing your Limiting Beliefs, you can begin to live a fuller life, and you can start taking apart your Inner Clutter.

Limiting Beliefs are a significant part of what makes up your Internal Clutter. However, they are not the only thing that can weigh heavy on your heart and block you from the Divine Flow of Abundance. It's time to talk about the fear factor…

Fears

The second main type of Internal Clutter is fear.

Fear is one of the most powerful emotions. It is a primal feeling. Different cultures have found unique ways of dealing with fear. One example is Halloween, a celebrated time of year when Americans mock fear-inducing creatures. Similarly, the way each of us deals with fear can take different forms. Some of us collect stuff to build a defensive layer against the outside world. Others develop ticks and superstitions. Whatever the external mechanism might be, fear is a form of Internal Clutter.

Fears make up a significant portion of your

Internal Clutter. Like Limiting Beliefs, Fear crumbles under scrutiny and acknowledgment. When you face your Fear, you can beat it!

How to Dispel Fear

Fear is a powerful enemy, but one that many people overcome on a daily basis. Fear has the same effects as Limiting Beliefs. It holds you down and holds you back. Fear can feel overwhelming at times, but it's something you can handle. Like Limiting Beliefs, you can organize and eliminate your fears through confrontation, and finding the opposite.

Imagine that Fear is one end of a pendulum at the height of its swing. On the other side of the pendulum lies Excitement, that sensation of eagerness to get out and see what the world has to offer. By acknowledging your Fears you allow the pendulum to swing to the other side. It swings back and forth throughout our lives, but what's important is being able to experience your Excitements and Fears without wallowing in either. The two extremes provide a healthy balance to our lives. A little fear is human, a lot of fear is crippling.

To organize your fears, the steps are similar to the ones we followed for Limiting Beliefs. Get your fears out in the open and acknowledge them. Practice Allowing the Now and do journaling and meditation to generate a list of fears. Once you've identified them, your fears will shrink.

Next, for each fear, find a way to rephrase it in terms of excitement. If you're afraid of something, it also means you're excited about something else. For example when I feel fear about getting on stage and speaking to a group of people, I acknowledge the butterflies in my stomach and instead focus on the excitement I feel about my message empowering them to change their lives.

When you acknowledge your Fear and react with Excitement, you will begin to break down your Internal Clutter. This might require a few tries, but that's okay. Don't lose your commitment. Like Limiting Beliefs, Fear can be conquered through the acknowledgement that there's nothing to be afraid of. When you face your Fears without judgment, you will take apart your Internal Clutter.

Fears and Limiting Beliefs are two of the main types of Inner Clutter, and both are significant. You have to acknowledge them, but also let them know they do not rule your life. Using techniques like Allowing the Now, the Happiness Seeking Missile, and the List of New Beliefs, you'll be able to address your Internal Clutter and begin your growth!

Now there's just one more piece of Inner Clutter you need to address, and this one is the hardest.

Repressed Trauma

Let me share a story to help illustrate how Trauma is a form a Clutter.

My neighbor, Phil, had a mother, Janelle, who adored music, especially when it was played live on her grand piano. The problem was, only her youngest daughter knew how to play the piano. Eventually the day came when her youngest daughter moved to a different state, and she didn't take the piano with her.

Unwilling to let the grand piano leave the family, Janelle pushed it on her oldest daughter who still lived nearby. She hoped that maybe one of her grandkids would pick up a love for the instrument.

The piano stayed with Janelle's oldest daughter for over a decade before she, too, moved out of state.

This left the grand piano in the hands of neighbor Phil, who still lived in the same town as Janelle.

Phil complained often about the piano. It took up so much space in his living room, no one ever played it, and his mother asked about it frequently even though she knew no one would be playing it. The real kicker for Phil was that he already had a keyboard that he never touched, stored away in his garage. The last thing he needed was a grand piano!

That piano stayed in Phil's living room for three years.

One day I walked outside to see a cube truck parked outside Phil's house and two burly men talking to Phil on his front porch. The side of the cube truck had the logo of a piano moving company. 45 minutes later the truck was gone, and I was ringing Phil's doorbell.

When Phil opened the door, his smile was ear to ear. "The piano's gone!" he practically sang.

I couldn't help myself. I asked, "Wow, and Janelle was okay with this?"

"Oh, she doesn't know, yet." Apparently a look of concern flashed across my face because Phil hurried to explain, "I called the high school choir and asked them if they wanted a grand piano for their practice room, and they said they'd take it."

This solution was ingenious, not only because it ensured the grand piano would get the respect and attention it deserved, but because Janelle lived right across the street from the high school. If she opened her window, she could probably hear the piano being played every day.

I later followed up with Phil to ask him how Janelle reacted when she found out about the grand piano's move. He said she was shocked, and initially sad, but once she realized that the piano and the piano's music would both be remaining in her life she was understanding.

Addressing Repressed Trauma

What does the story of Janelle's grand piano have to say about Trauma? Remember, External

Clutter mirrors Internal Clutter. Trauma is a grand piano sized burden placed in your memory. It grabs at your attention, but the energy required to deal with it is often more than you can handle on your own, so you ignore it. Over time, the Trauma becomes Repressed, and eventually you let it become attached to your identity.

The truth is, though, that Repressed Trauma does not define you. And when the weight of it is lifted from your mind, the light of the Divine Energy will come rushing in to fill that space.

In order to lift the weight of Repressed Trauma, two needs must be met: specialized professionals and creative problem solving.

Seek Professional Help

Trauma is an injury. It might be invisible, but it is no less real than a broken leg. Your psyche, like your body, can suffer injuries, and sometimes the injuries require specialized doctors to aid in the healing process. When you don't seek the help of professionals, collateral damage can ensue as you try to remove the Trauma on your own.

Imagine if Phil had tried to move the piano out of his living room all by himself. At the very least, he might have scratched up his floor, broken a wheel on the piano, and messed up the tuning. Worst case scenario, that piano could have fallen and crushed him. By seeking the help of professional piano movers, Phil not only removed the grand piano from his living room safely, but was able to realize the instrument's potential positivity for others at the high school.

The Repressed Trauma you may be carrying is its own beast. Clinical psychiatrists can specialize in specific types of psychiatric care in the same way surgeons can specialize in operating on specific parts of the body. If you know the type of Trauma you have suffered, don't hesitate or be ashamed to seek out professional help to address whatever is weighing on you.

When you have the support and confidence that your Trauma can be lifted and moved, and potentially reframed for good, a whole world will open up for you to begin creative problem solving.

Be Free to Be Creative

The hardest part of addressing Repressed Trauma is committing to dealing with it. Like the grand piano, Trauma can sit around for years before you finally make a decision about it. Often, the only reason you keep repressing it is because it is big, heavy, and intimidating. But once you commit to moving it and secure professional help, you are free to tap into its potential energy.

Remember, all clutter has potential energy. The potential energy of Repressed Trauma is like a reservoir contained by a dam. You don't want the dam to burst, but you do want the dam to tap into the potential energy of the water. When Phil committed to hiring the professional piano movers, he was free to access the potential positive energy of the instrument beyond his living room. He saw a need in his community, and refocused the piano's energy to serve that need.

Whatever Traumas you have suffered, you probably aren't the only one familiar with that pain. When you commit to addressing Repressed Trauma with a specialized professional, you free up the potential energy to safely serve others. When other victims of similar Trauma see the light of the Divine Energy shining through you, they will be encouraged to believe their Trauma is not immobilizing either.

Repressed Trauma is the heaviest of all Internal Clutter, and is often the primary driving force behind all External Clutter. If you don't believe your Trauma can be moved, I challenge you to consider that as a Limiting Belief and make a List of New Beliefs. If you are too afraid of your Trauma to even think about looking at it, take some deep breaths and make a List of New Beliefs for turning that fear into excitement. Then seek professional help and creatively tap into the immense potential for positivity that is within you!

Conclusion

Organizing your Internal Clutter can seem like a daunting prospect. With External Clutter, you can lift boxes, give away items, and see clear markers of improvement in your life. As you begin to tackle Internal Clutter, there are fewer visible signs. However, the progress can mean so much more. Through overcoming your beliefs and fears, you can become the best version of yourself. When you clean out your Internal Clutter, your life will improve as you reconnect with the Divine Flow of Abundance.

Internal Clutter is composed of Limiting Beliefs, Fears, and Repressed Trauma. All of these build within you, but they are lies about who you are and how you are supposed to be in the world. You have the capacity to overcome the factors that hold you down. Through direct confrontation and consistency, employing practices like the List of New Beliefs, and specialized professional help, you can let your Limiting Beliefs, Fears, and Traumas know they don't hold power over you. You are the driver of your mind and you have the capability to bring it under control. As you address your Limiting Beliefs and Fears, you begin to tackle the clutter that's built up inside of you.

Being happy is your birthright. As you clear your Internal Clutter, you will see that the things you worried about in the past were simply that: worries. Through reflection, acknowledgment, and consistent effort, you can overcome your Inner Clutter and bring yourself closer to the Divine Flow of Abundance!

Conclusion

Cleaning Up the Rest

We all have clutter built up in our environments. For you it might be the drawer full of unused pens next to your stove, the row of unworn jackets in your closet, or the thousands of unread emails in your inbox. Clutter shows itself in a variety of ways. The items we collect, and the messes we choose to ignore, protect us from Inner Clutter we don't want to deal with.

In the beginning of this book, I asked one question: What's the secret to decluttering your life? Decluttering is more than pulling out garbage bags and finding your nearest donation center. The clutter you're holding onto in your physical life represents all the accumulated clutter in your emotional life. The things you cling to serve as blockage, shielding you from the turmoil within that you don't want to address.

The truth of Physical Clutter reflecting the mental state is commonly known in our society, yet we don't do anything about it. The internationally watched TV show South Park ran an episode where one of the side characters, the school counselor, worked in an office filled to the ceiling with papers and cups. When the main characters looked into his habits, they saw that he had repressed a memory from his childhood where he was sexually abused. From the mainstream media to peer-reviewed articles, many are aware of the link between external accumulation and internal repression.

Your clutter isn't solely physical, it's the accumulation of everything you are going through and every worry you have. However, your situation is not insurmountable. No matter how much clutter you have, it can be cleaned!

Review:

Clutter appears in many different ways, often manifesting as something we like or appreciate, which hides the fact that something deeper is present. External Clutter accumulates on and around us in order to protect us from facing our true traumas. The main forms are:

1. Physical Clutter, the most commonly cited form, is about your possessions. For you that might be a drawer of pens, piles of junk you haven't had the strength to get rid of, the garage you can't park your car in, or a meticulously organized collection you can't part with. Physical Clutter takes up space in your life that could be filled by anything else. When this form of clutter surrounds you, you tend to make excuses, not accepting that its presence indicates much more than meets the eye.
2. Digital Clutter shows up on your screens and hard drives. Whether it appears for you as thousands of unread emails in your inbox, a deluge of files acting as a labyrinth on your desktop, or scanned essays and papers stretching back through your college

days, Digital Clutter can put pressure on your mind through its immensity. Holding onto things you don't need is detrimental to your health. On the screen, it's so easy to let things build up and never realize you're drowning.

3. Body Clutter shows up on your physical frame. Your body is the vessel you must live in and taking good care of it allows you to live to your fullest potential. Overeating, undereating, and other bodily stress often indicates that there's something else going on. The way you treat your body reveals your inner pain. If you won't show respect to yourself physically, it's a sign of inner disrespect as well.

You must free yourself from all three forms of External Clutter, but that's easier said than done. The clutter you can see and touch masks a deeper clutter, Internal Clutter, which forms from the traumas, fears, and encounters you have accumulated from the day you were born. This collected build-up within your mind restricts you from finding happiness and clearing the Physical Clutter. Without first addressing Internal Clutter, you won't find true health and wellness.

Internal Clutter is formed through traumatic experiences you might wish to forget. Abuses, both physical and mental, cause trauma in your life. The circumstances you are born into may have created Internal Clutter, with the stresses of your environment putting unique pressures on your shoulders. Family strife, such as divorce or death, are other ways in which trauma is created. You have Internal Clutter, and only addressing your External Clutter is not a lasting solution.

All the Clutter in our lives is connected. So how do we begin to heal?

You can address your clutter with a few simple practices. Allowing the Now will help you recognize the emotions coming into your mind, not pushing down feelings, but letting them come in and out like visitors. The Happiness Seeking Missile will encourage you to break from the constant stream of negativity around you and look for the silver linings in every situation, no matter how hard they might be to find. The Divine Flow of Abundance is waiting for you, and your recognition of its power is the first step towards healing. These techniques are simple, but effective, and offer a brighter light on the road ahead.

What's great about these forms of healing through meditation is that you are capable of incorporating them into your life no matter your circumstances. There are no outside pressures telling you not to live this way. Being conscious of the emotions within and the world around is how you'll begin to reframe your mind and start seeing the good first. Through these simple techniques, you will begin to break down your Internal Clutter.

When the Internal Clutter breaks down, the External has no choice but to go along with it. As you come to peace with yourself, you'll notice the spaces in your life that need improvement. You'll shed the extra pounds you've wanted to lose. You'll organize your inbox into a working system that's easy to follow. You'll be putting loose items in bags and clearing the clutter unconsciously in no time. The External is impacted by the Internal; it's all connected, and your life will take a turn for the better when you see that relationship!

The Easy Truth

When you think of making a life change, your mind often jumps to the difficulty, not the benefits.

You tend to lament the journey and not draw inspiration from the destination. In the end, however, clearing the clutter is worth it. I went from being addicted to crack and contemplating suicide to actively enjoying every moment and striving to improve lives on a daily basis. I'm taking apart my clutter piece by piece alongside many others.

There are hiccups, but you can't expect growth to be linear. Reflecting on your life, confronting difficult feelings, and rejoining the Divine Flow through taking apart your clutter is a constant process. However, in all that, there is the bliss of no pressure. Your growth and development rests on your own shoulders, this process is not one you do for others. This is a conscious bettering of the self, one which we are all capable of achieving.

In 2004, I was experiencing my first few years of sobriety and helping others clear the clutter in their lives. At the same time, Maynor De Leon decided to make a change. Maynor, weighing at the time over 700 pounds, began to work out and eat right in order to save his own life. At the time I'm writing this, Maynor weighs slightly over 400 pounds and is a social media star.

I heard about Maynor through a friend and have been following his journey. Every day, he posts his workout, communicates his story, and pushes others to find inspiration to better themselves. Maynor achieved this massive weight loss not through surgery, diet pills, or anything of the like. Instead, he ate clean and has consistently worked out, seven days a week, pushing himself to be the man he knows he can be.

On his page, Maynor occasionally posts a photo of himself at his heaviest. In the picture, he smiles up at the camera, holding a large sheet cake. Underneath that smile, though, is a deep well of depression and a man who contemplated taking his own life. Maynor speaks to how traumas in childhood pushed him to become 700 pounds and how he has to face those traumas along his path to his desired weight.

In 2019, Nike took notice of Maynor's journey. Looking to expand their brand into more than traditional professional and Olympic athletes, the sports behemoth made a commercial tailored around his journey. The video has been viewed millions of times and Maynor's story has spread around the globe. I believe this is because we all see ourselves in his struggle and in his triumphs.

Over the course of this book, I've underscored that anyone can change their life. However, if big changes are so easy to make, then why doesn't everyone? Think about how many gyms are filled on January 1st compared to June 3rd of the same year. The major challenge in your way is consistency. My story, Maynor's story, and this entire book all underscore the fact that you can absolutely do it if you make a plan and stick to it.

Consistency is the hard part. Changing your lifestyle requires strength. While you may slip sometimes, the road is a long one, and you need to keep walking. The journey becomes easier with every step you take!

We all have clutter inside and outside of ourselves in some form. Some of us attempt to avoid facing it through food, others through drugs, others through collecting objects. However, in the end, you must approach your emotions head-on to live your life to the fullest. The Divine Flow of Abundance is waiting for you to recognize your great potential.

Two Choices

I have confidence you could take everything covered in this book, go on your own, put it all into action, and get results that you previously thought to be impossible. I am certain that left to your own devices, resources, time, and effort, you can make a go at this in a way most people will never be able to.

And if that were your only option, it would be a worthy ideal to pursue.

But what if there were another option? An option that allowed us to go at this together. A chance to go deeper than we already have in this speed-read of a book. What if I played an active, ongoing role in your results, took responsibility for your success, and had an obligation to your outcome? How would that make this journey different for you?

Do you think I could empower you with any and all resources at my disposal to stack the deck in your favor and make success all but inevitable? What if I had shortcuts, support systems, and additional insights that go even deeper into getting you the results you want, desire, and deserve? If I had such an option for you, would you love to hear more about it and what it could do for you?

I would love to tell you all about this potential, and I'm offering you One Free 1-on-1 Coaching Call with me to hear all about it. All you have to do is email me at info@declutteringspaces.com and tell me you want the "One Free Coaching Call" offer from this book.

It would be my honor to come alongside you for your decluttering journey.

Printed in Great Britain
by Amazon

67932610R00098